TITANIC
VALOUR

324

Senator Bourne: Did Officer Lowe call for volunteers to return to the wreck?

Mr. Crow: No, sir; he impressed upon us that we must go back to the wreck.

From evidence given by Titanic *crewman George Crowe at the 1912 Congressional Subcommittee investigation into the* Titanic *disaster*

I have never prided myself upon being a prophet, but of this I am positive: When the Titanic disaster has become a matter of history, Harold G. Lowe will occupy the hero's place. The reason is that in you were combined the qualities of Courage, Firmness and Good Judgement.

None of your brother officers lacked courage, but your exceptional demonstration of the latter qualities will mark you as the one who secured the results. In this country at least we honour most the man who gets results.

Sheriff Joseph E Bayliss, Sergeant at Arms to the United States Senate, 20 May 1912

TO TASIA, 5/10/15
DENISE & GARY FRANCIS IN
ENGLAND SENT US THIS BOOK
TO SHARE WITH YOU AND YOUR
FAMILY. WE HOPE YOU ENJOY
THIS STORY ABOUT THE TITANIC
FROM SUE SUE & DAN

TITANIC VALOUR

THE LIFE OF FIFTH OFFICER
HAROLD LOWE

INGER SHEIL

The History Press

For my parents Sandra and Ted Sheil

Who taught me to love the sea, but to never turn my
back on it

Front cover photographs: Lowe Family Collection (John Lowe) and Steve Hall.

Back cover photograph: Lowe Family Collection (John Lowe).

First published 2012

The History Press
The Mill, Brimscombe Port
Stroud, Gloucestershire, GL5 2QG
www.thehistorypress.co.uk

British Library Cataloguing in Publication Data.
A catalogue record for this book is available from the British Library.

ISBN 978 0 7524 6996 6

Typesetting and origination by The History Press
Printed in Great Britain
Manufacturing managed by Jellyfish Print Solutions Ltd

CONTENTS

Acknowledgements

Reading works on the most famous shipwreck of all, the loss of the RMS *Titanic*, one name kept appearing. It seemed that whenever something interesting was being said or done during this unfolding disaster and its aftermath, Harold Lowe was involved. I looked in vain for a complete biography of this colourful individual – none existed. The fragments in secondary sources about his life before and after the sinking were sketchy at best. So I embarked on a journey to find out the truth about this intriguing man, and found not only supporters along the way, but friends.

This book would not have been possible without the support and encouragement of Harold G. Lowe's descendants. Harold's son, Harold William George Lowe, was receptive to the idea and in turn introduced me to his children, Godfrey and Gerri, and his nephew John Lowe. It is said that families can be the enemy of biographers, but in the Lowe family I found allies of the very best kind. Harold W.G. Lowe wrote to me in an early letter that 'all I would seek is accuracy. I would not want [my father] to receive any more praise or blame than is his due.' It is a spirit of which his father would have approved, and which all the family has demonstrated. While doing their utmost to help with information and suggestions, no member of the family has ever sought to dictate the narrative or direction of this book. Sadly, Harold W.G. Lowe passed away before seeing the work completed – I hope it would have fulfilled his hopes for it.

In North Wales I met Captain John Lowe and his wife Cara, who have more than once extended their warm hospitality and have gone far beyond any call of duty to make their family archive accessible and facilitate the necessary research. John, with his background in the mercantile marine, has provided invaluable insight into his profession. Godfrey Lowe and his wife Bernie generously shared information as we explored Barmouth and travelled to Llandudno and Deganwy together and have been continuously supportive.

I value all these friendships very much. Other members of the family, including Harold W.G. Lowe's wife Peggy Lowe, Janet Lowe and Harold G. Lowe's nephew John Lowe (son of Arthur Lowe) have also contributed immeasurably, as did Barbara Whitehouse who shared her childhood memories of the Lowe family in Deganwy.

My good friend Kerri Sundberg was a major inspiration for this project and this book owes much to her talent and passion for the subject. *Titanic* author David Bryceson has been an ongoing source of support, and kindly gave me his extensive correspondence with Harold W.G. Lowe about his father.

Author and researcher Senan Molony has been a fount of practical support, providing extensive input into this book's final form, for which I am very grateful as much as I am for his constant urgings to publish. John Creamer has been exceptionally generous with use of images and permission to quote from documents in his collection.

It is a matter of great regret for me that this book was not completed before Ted Dowding (nephew of *Titanic* survivor Clear Cameron) and his wife Dinah passed away. They were dear friends, and kindly gave me permission to quote from their book *Clear to America by Titanic and Beyond*, a collection of letters by his aunt and her friend, Nellie Walcroft.

The following individuals – researchers, authors and the relatives of those who sailed – made this work possible: Jenni Atkinson, Mark Baber, Stephen Cameron, Miriam Cannell MBE, Mark Chirnside, Alex Churchill, Andrew Clarkson, Pat Cook, Mary Conlon, Kate Dornan, Ted and Dinah Dowding, David Fletcher-Rogers, Christine Geyer, Phil Gowan, David Haisman, Steve Hall, Olga Hill, Phil Hind, Ben Holme, Tom Hughes, Daniel Klistorner, Roseanne Macintyre, Ilya McVey, Fiona Nitschke, Andrew Rogers, Bill Sauder, Eric Sauder, Monika Simon, Parks Stephenson, Brian Ticehurst, Mike Tennaro, Geoff Whitfield, Mary-Louise Williams and Pat Winship.

I am also deeply indebted to the staff of the following institutions and organisations: my colleagues at the Australian National Maritime Museum, the Bayliss Public Library, the British Titanic Society, the Colindale Newspaper Archives, the Gwynedd Archives, the Encyclopaedia Titanica messageboard, The National Maritime Museum (UK), the Liverpool Archives, the National Archives (UK), The Memorial University of Newfoundland Maritime History Archive, the Royal Naval Museum, The Provincial Grand Lodge of

North Wales, Southampton Archives, The Titanic Historical Society, the Titanic-Titanic messageboard and the staff of The History Press.

Finally, my own 'flotilla': Rebecca, Cameron, Lachlan, Gabrielle and Kieran Bryant; Edward Sheil; Alison Fahy; Jill, Glyn and Nicholas Raines; and my parents Ted and Sandra, to whom this book is dedicated.

PROLOGUE

When RMS *Titanic* took her 2½-mile plunge to the ocean floor, she left behind her on the surface a slight haze, strewn bits of wreckage, and many hundreds of screaming men, women and children.

The last lifeboat successfully launched had left the ship shortly after 2 a.m., pulling away into the dark. Still aboard the *Titanic* were some 1,500 people. These were soon plunged into the 29°F water, where they began freezing to death. Their cries would haunt the 712 survivors in the encircling lifeboats for the rest of their lives. They were 'terrible cries', 'awful cries, and yelling and shouting.'

A few of those in the water crawled aboard two canvas-sided lifeboats, so-called 'collapsibles', which had floated free from the boat deck as the ship sank. Balancing on the keel of Collapsible 'B', which had overturned during attempts at launch, or up to their knees in the freezing water of swamped boat 'A', they were only marginally better off than those in the water.

For most, rescue would not be forthcoming. Entire families perished that night in the pitiless North Atlantic. The Goodwins (father, mother and six children), who had hoped to settle in Niagara Falls, were swept away by the cataract. All eleven members of the Sage family, travelling third class like the Goodwins, were obliterated. The Rice family from Ireland, the Anderssons from Sweden – all died.

The lifeboats waiting out in the darkness were almost all underfilled. With their total capacity for 1,178 people, at least 466 places went unoccupied. The few in the boats listened in fear and anguish. They did not go back.

In Boat 1 fireman Charles Hendrickson broached the question of returning. The idea met with a lukewarm reception, and no attempt was made. In Boat 6 the ladies implored Quartermaster Robert Hichens to return. He announced: 'It's our lives now, not theirs.'

Fourth Officer Boxhall lit a flare in Boat 2 and the volume of shrieks briefly swelled up louder than before. Third Officer Pitman, in command of Boat 5, declared, 'Now, men, we will pull toward the wreck', but 'very nearly all' the passengers objected, fearing for their lives. Pitman then ordered his men to lay by their oars, and Boat 5 continued to drift, its occupants listening to the 'crying, shouting, moaning'.

Able Seaman Fred Clench told the people in his boat the voices came from men in the other lifeboats, shouting to each other so they did not get lost in the darkness. For one survivor, the howls seemed to 'go on forever'. Pitman estimated 'a continual moan for about an hour'. Then the voices died away from the dark Atlantic's surface, and one by one fell to silence.

Some distance away from the mass of people, a young ship's officer had been rounding up as many lifeboats as he could find in the gloom of the moonless night. Tying together lifeboats 14, 4, 12 and Collapsible 'D', he told them: 'All right, consider the whole of you under my orders; remain with me.'

While the people in other boats rowed, sang to drown out the cries, or simply sat deaf to the final nightmare, the officer had been busy transferring passengers out of Boat 14 to prepare a return to pick up survivors. He waited until the moment he could safely return without endangering his handful of crew.

Now, he judged, the moment had come. Harold Godfrey Lowe, fifth officer of RMS *Titanic*, turned to those under his charge and told them they were going back.

CHAPTER 1

'WHERE ARE
YOU BOUND?'

Composed and apparently fearless in the face of loud and threatening voices, Hannah Lowe rode into the crowd that surrounded John Wesley. The mob had every intention of stoning the preacher for the crime of delivering a sermon out of doors. This practice faced bitter opposition in these early days of Methodism, and encounters between the evangelicals and their opponents often led to more than a clash of words. Hannah, distant great-aunt of a *Titanic* officer, was no stranger to this threat of mob violence; her father, George Lowe, was one of Wesley's staunchest supporters and had helped him establish chapels in Chester. Now Hannah stood as the only obstacle between the angry local men and the target of their wrath. An accomplished equestrienne, she placed her horse and herself between Wesley and the riotous throng and surveyed them coolly.

'The first stone at the preacher will come through me,' she announced.

The crowd, nonplussed at first, distracted, lost its purpose. It gradually dispersed under Hannah's watchful eye, leaving Wesley unharmed. Or so ran the legend.

Nestled in the shadow of the Welsh mountain Cader Idris, by the mouth of the river Mawddach, Barmouth remains today much as it was in previous centuries. The picturesque community is one of the towns and hamlets girdling a stretch of the coast in the thin border between the hills and the sea. Said to be the seat of Idris the Giant, legend has it that anyone sleeping overnight on the mountain will awake either a madman or a poet. The town's buildings extend in tiers up the lower slopes, the natural barrier to the inland emphasising the sea alone as the sustainer of Barmouth's people, from the once-thriving shipwrights and fishermen, to the bed-and-breakfast trade today.

Barmouth had been home to a busy shipbuilding industry. In the mid-eighteenth century it was counted asone of the major ports of Wales, but by the 1840s two major factors converged to ensure its decline. The development of Porthmadoc to the north as a shipping centre, and the emergence of the railway in coastal transport and trade combined to radically alter the town's economic base.

The railway worked both ways. Although the town's history as a sea bathing resort dated to 1766, for the first time holidaymakers from industrial centres inland could avail themselves of easy access to the coast. The Barmouth of the second half of the nineteenth century adapted to a seasonal influx of holidaymakers.

The small resort town's natural beauty, where even the buildings seem hewn out of the grey stone of the hills, may be what drew George Lowe. His artist's eye must have seen the bare-canvass potential of ocean, estuary and clouded mountain peaks. He would paint these scenes many times in the years to come. George Lowe, from the line of fearless Hannah Lowe, selected a site on the southern approach to the town, a patch of land halfway up the hill with views far inland along the Mawddach estuary. The land dropped away sharply where he would build a house for his family, straight down to the estuary, with ready access to the river and tidal flats that fringed the Irish Sea. With walls several feet thick in places to withstand the Welsh winters, the house was substantial inside, being some three storeys over a basement. It was named Penrallt, Welsh for 'House on the Slope'.

Harold Lowe was born, raised and died in Wales. His family origins, however, were neither Welsh nor Celtic, although his ancestors came from just over the Marches in Cheshire, England. The legend was that they could trace their ancestry to one of William the Conqueror's men, Hugh D'Avranches, better known to history as Hugh Lupus, Hugh the Wolf.

He had been made Earl of Chester in 1069 for his part in suppressing the rebellious Welsh. To the Welsh he was Hugh Vras – 'Hugh the fat' – whose gluttony made him so obese that he could hardly walk. Yet it was also said that, fat or no, he also fathered a number of illegitimate children.

Harold Lowe's faith in the family's connection with the waddling, swaddling Earl of Chester would be demonstrated through his use of a heraldic device – the snarling wolf – that signified Hugh Lupus. But the first firm foundations for his line can be traced to 1589 when the Lowes were simple farmers at Guilden Sutton, Cheshire. Their connection with farming continued until the latter part of the eighteenth century, when George Lowe (1738–1814), father of Hannah Lowe, became a successful miller and flour dealer. A Freeman of Chester, his sons George and Edward became a silversmith and clockmaker respectively. The thread of these occupations passed down through generations, and for over a century the Lowes found their calling as skilled artisans.

George Edward Lowe was born in Chester on 20 April 1848. It was the year of revolutionary upheaval in Europe; appropriate for the boy who would grow up to be somewhat unconventional. It had seemed that he would follow in the footsteps of his father, his earliest described profession being that of goldsmith or jeweller and watchmaker. There is some suggestion that the family cultivated artistic connections; the 1881 census listed a young artist, Walter Deken, as a visitor to the Lowe household. George Lowe was of a somewhat flamboyant, even bohemian character, and rather than continue the family tradition of metalwork and clockmaking, he was drawn to painting, and oils in particular. Yet for many years he would continue to list his occupation as 'jeweller and watchmaker', being a member of the family firm of Lowe & Sons, with shops in Chester, Llandudno and Liverpool.

George met Emma Harriet Quick when he was working in the Liverpool shop. Harriet, as she preferred to be known, was a local girl, born in Liverpool on 24 March 1856, the youngest of Anne Theresa and Thomas Lethbridge Quick's four children. Thomas Quick was a district police superintendent, a comparatively new occupation. The 'New Police' had only been formed in 1836 as a result of Robert Peel's Municipal Corporations Act (1835), which also gave rise to the popular colloquialism 'peelers'. Thomas, originally from Merton in Devonshire, had served with the Metropolitan force before being reassigned to the Liverpool dock force. He saw lively service in the early days of the Liverpool police, when rows and riots were almost a daily occurrence on the docks. The dock force was later amalgamated into the town force, and he was appointed a borough superintendent. He was a man of considerable personal courage, in keeping with his occupation, and it is recorded that he once imperilled his life to save men trapped in a burning building. His wife Anne, whose parents were of some means, was a Liverpool girl. A brief, elusive description of her 'loving heart and constant tenderness' is virtually all that survives of her reputation; she predeceased her husband.[1]

Hannah grew up with her siblings Thomas, Elizabeth and Robert at the police station in Olive Street where they lived with the

Bridewell keeper, his family and several servants. The children could not help but be aware of the cast of characters that came and went in the station: the innocent, the unfortunate, and the denizens of Liverpool's underworld. There was early tragedy in Hannah's life; her mother had already passed away when her father, who had suffered from heart disease for years, suffered a stroke in mid-1867 resulting in partial paralysis. On 4 December 1867 he suffered another stroke and passed away at their home in Everton, where the family had moved following his retirement. There was more sorrow to come when Thomas' oldest child and namesake, banker's clerk Thomas Lethbridge Quick Junior – fifteen years older than Harriet – began exhibiting what were diagnosed as the symptoms of insanity. The younger Thomas died of phthisis on 7 August 1872, barely a month after his admission to the Ashton Street Lunatic Asylum.

Hannah remains a rather elusive figure, beyond such shadowy details as her preference for her middle name. How she met and became enamoured of George Lowe remains obscure, but on 6 June 1877, when she had just passed her twenty-first birthday, Harriet married her charming beau. Initially they set up house in Llandudno, North Wales, with a single maidservant. Their son George Ernest Lowe, first of what was to be a large family, was born in 1878. A daughter, Ada Florence, followed in 1879. In 1882 George and Harriet – now pregnant with their third child – moved into George's father's home, 'Bryn Lupus', in Eglwysrhos, a stepping-stone to Barmouth.

It was in his grandfather's home that Harold Godfrey Lowe was born on 21 November 1882. The date and place of birth are established beyond doubt, but for a time in his life the future *Titanic* officer was either uncertain or dissembling these details. As late as 1910 some documents would record his year of birth as 1883, and the place as Liverpool.

Although they left Bryn Lupus while he was still a baby, the name of his grandfather's home struck a family chord. The name 'Bryn Lupus' translates as 'Wolf Hill'. Many years later, after his own retirement, Harold Lowe had stained-glass panels set into the door of his home with the slavering wolves of Hugh D'Avranches.

The young family moved more than once in these early years of Harold's life. By 1884, George, now describing himself as simply an 'artist', had set up residence with Harriet and brood at Bronwen Terrace, Harlech. Between Portmadoc in the north and Barmouth to the south, Harlech had prospered around a castle, built by

England's Edward I as part of a ring of fortresses intended to subdue the rebellious Welsh.

The Lowe family continued to expand with rapidity. Another daughter, Annie May, was followed by Edgar Reginald, born on 20 September 1884. Harold and Edgar's proximity in age – just two years – was reflected in their closeness as they grew up. Both were fated to go to sea.

First there was Barmouth. By 1893 George Lowe took his family on their final move, to Penrallt, the House on the Slope, scene of an idyllic childhood on the edge of Tremadoc Bay.

Tremadoc had a fierce reputation. In March 1893 the SS *Glendarroch*, out of London for Liverpool, ran aground on St Patrick's Causeway. The Barmouth lifeboat successfully rescued all the crew, as it would again just five weeks later when the ketch *Canterbury Bell* was wrecked in identical circumstances.

In 1895 the causeway almost claimed the four-masted barge *Andrada* that was beached for several days. In August that year the Barmouth and Pwllheli lifeboats laid out anchors from the stranded barque *Kragero* when she ran aground in rough seas and a south-westerly gale.

The boy Harold Lowe, like other residents of Barmouth, would have been well aware of these dramatic incidents and rescues. He was learning the perils of seafaring, while also becoming fired and inspired by the actions of ordinary men in lifeboats facing grave personal danger to save the lives of others.

Although the heyday of Barmouth as a centre for shipping was over, coastal ships and tramps still arrived with regularity. Nautical themes entered George Lowe's work, and subjects such as the coaster SS *Dora* featured in his paintings. For the Lowe boys, the sea was both an educator and an entertainer. In time, it would become a livelihood. In years to come it would also take a cruel toll on the Lowe family and it never ceased to be an integral part of their lives.

Lessons in the crafts of the sea began early, with long hours spent along the river, the estuary and out to sea, fishing. The oldest boy, George Junior, used his punt to carry people across the river Mawddach. His younger brothers tagged along and would come to know his circle of friends, the other boatmen who worked the same trade.

Visitors who took to the boats or indulged in sea bathing were not always water wise, and the estuary and seafront were hazardous.

Tuesday 7 August 1894 saw Barmouth in the full swing of the summer season. Visitors poured into the resort, took walks up in the hills to the Panorama lookout, and hired boats on the Mawddach. Pleasure-seekers and townsfolk alike were shocked out of the holiday mood when the estuary, living up to its dangerous reputation, claimed several lives in the worst accident in the collective memory. A party of visitors, members of the National Home Reading Unit, hired three local boats to take them up the estuary to Bontddu, and then planned to return with the outgoing tide.

One boatman refused to hire his boats to the party as he felt the tides were too dangerous. Another, William Jones, required considerable persuasion before agreeing to take out his boat out. One of the other vessels was in the charge of a local boatman, Lewis Edwards, while a third group was led by Oxford University student Percival Gray, who felt himself accustomed enough to rowing. Several of Gray's friends intended to accompany the group, but felt that the river was too rough and the wind too strong. More than one boatman on the quay advised them not to go.

The party arrived safely upriver in spite of a strong out-flowing tide. On the return, with the wind blowing fiercely enough to dislodge the hats on the heads of two of the men in Jones' boat, a wave caught the craft broadside on and instantly capsized her. Jones was able to swim ashore to commandeer another boat, the *Pearl*, for rescue work. On his return to the site, he managed to pull five of his seven passengers into the boat.

Of the other two boats, Lewis Edwards was able to safely land his passengers ashore. He then journeyed to the *Pearl*, where one of the women pulled from the water had already succumbed to hypothermia. Searching for the third boat, the men heard screams from the far off mid-river.

About a mile from the scene of the original mishap they found a woman, Miss Packer, clinging to a seat in the water. There were no other survivors from her vessel, that commanded by the student, Gray.

Robert Morris, one of the rescuers, described what they found:

> I saw the body of a lady. She was dead. I lifted her up, and with help placed the body in the boat. We saw the body of another lady, dead, and in the river, and carried it to the boat. Ten yards further we saw a body of a gentleman. We fetched another boat and near this boat there was the body of another gentleman, and we put it in the boat.

We crossed the river to help Lewis Edwards to carry the bodies of another gentleman and a lady. Then William Jones saw the body of another lady in the water, and we placed it in the boat. We waited until the police came there. We had seven bodies.[2]

The county coroner convened an inquest the following afternoon. George Lowe Senior, Harold's father, was appointed jury foreman. In his presence eight men were placed in one of the boats to test its seaworthiness and evidence was collected from the boatmen, survivors and those who had decided not to join the fatal expedition.

After 40 minutes' deliberation, George Lowe returned the jury's verdict. They found that each of the total of ten dead had been drowned though the swamping of a boat. They made several recommendations concerning the number of passengers to be carried in boats, the inclusion of a skilled boatman in each craft, and called for an inspector to warn people of the danger they incurred in boating on the estuary under conditions like those on the day of the accident.

The jury was unanimous in commending the actions of Jones after the accident, and of Edwards in landing his passengers and returning to assist. The details of the events that took place that summer day, the tragic deaths and the attempts of the boatmen to rescue the victims, would have a profound effect on the small community. Whether or not George Lowe discussed in any detail the evidence he had heard with his family, Harold was old enough to have heard for himself the mixture of facts and rumours surrounding what had happened out on the Mawddach.

The lives of George Lowe and his family were to be even more directly touched by a boating accident the following year. With Christmas just past and the New Year still to come, at teatime on Friday 27 December 1895, George Lowe Junior took his punt from where it was moored in Aberamffra Bay across the mouth of the estuary to Penrhyn Point, and then crossed back to Aberamffra. Later that evening, at about 5.30, he left the house to secure the punt, apparently in 'good health and good spirits'. What happened next is a matter of conjecture.

The evidence submitted at the coroner's inquest suggests that he missed his footing as he descended the quay to get into the punt and was pitched into the sea. Unlike his younger brother Harold, boatman George could not swim. His sister Ada raised the alarm between

9 and 10 p.m. The family first searched the grounds of Penrallt, and
going down to Aberamffra could see the punt in what seemed its
usual position. As the Lowes continued their late-night search
through the town, one of George's friends had an eerie experience.

Robert Morris, a boatman involved in the rescue efforts of the
previous summer, was awakened about 1.30 on Saturday morning
by someone knocking at the door. He and his brother came down
to answer the summons, only to find themselves gazing into the
empty night.

Morris, as he later told the inquest, could not shake the feeling that
there was something wrong. Walking down the street he found Ada
and Annie Lowe near the Barmouth Hotel, who told him that George
was missing. Ada believed some mishap had occurred with the boat.

Morris went to Aberamffra. He could see George's boat alongside
the quay, attached by a single rope. Going to another vantage point,
he spotted a body in about 3½ft of water. Morris' brother Francis
now arrived on the scene with Dr Lloyd and a boatman.

They stalked across George Lowe's small punt to a larger boat
from which they were in position to reach the floating corpse. While
the other men balanced the boat Morris stretched out far and pulled
the body in with a mussel rake.

PC Barnard, hastily summoned by Francis Morris, hurried up.
The men moved the body onto a stretcher and then to the quay
where Dr Lloyd examined it and found no wounds or bruises. Life
had apparently been extinct for some five or six hours.

The men and distraught family members took George Lowe back
to Penrallt. There were perhaps shades of Ham Peggotty in *David
Copperfield,* with the drowned boatman being carried to the house
after he was washed back to shore. That same afternoon an inquest
was held at the police station. After viewing the body in the family
home, the jury returned to hear evidence from Ada, Morris, Lloyd
and Barnard. A verdict of 'accidentally drowned' was returned, and a
vote of condolence passed for the bereaved family.

George Ernest Lowe had been a popular young man, known for his
'gentle and sympathetic manners', and his death was said to have
'cast quite a heavy gloom over the neighbourhood'. The Victorian
rituals of grieving were observed, the black-bordered mourning
cards distributed to friends and relatives to mark his passing, and
with a rector officiating at the house and graveside, a procession

wound its way from Penrallt to Llanaber churchyard in several car-
riages. In spite of the heavy rain there was a large attendance of
George's friends, including many boatmen and choirboys who sang
with 'great feeling and efficiency'.[3]

What the thirteen-year-old Harold Lowe felt at the loss of his
brother can only be imagined. Typically circumspect in discussing his
own emotions, when speaking later about the event he would refer
to the tremendous shock the death of an eldest son and namesake
caused his father, who deeply mourned the loss. But Harold too felt
distress and grief at the sudden bereavement, the severed happiness.
His older brother, who had left the house hours before in the height
of health and spirits, was carried home ice cold and still. George had
been a skilled boatman, well liked and gregarious, only seventeen
years old. Without warning, he had been snatched by the sea. It was a
lesson the quick and impressionable adolescent Harold did not forget,
but it did not prevent his testing himself against the same elements.

Given his later career and *Titanic* association, it should come as no
surprise that the earliest anecdotes of Harold Lowe centre on childhood exploits involving boats. The first recorded incident took place
out at sea, with what might easily have been fatal results. On the afternoon of 14 September 1896, Harold took his father's punt out from
Aberamffra for a sail. It was, so the *Barmouth Advertiser* noted, 'rather a
risky thing to do considering his youth and the squally weather.'

When about half a mile out from shore, thirteen-year-old Lowe
was struck by the boom and the boat capsized. Fully clothed
and wearing heavy boots, he swam ashore and was, according to
the *Advertiser*, 'none the worse save for the wetting'. The incident
entered local lore, to be recalled by Barmouth residents many years
later after Harold had passed through another ordeal at sea.

The episode with the punt demonstrated his stubborn perse-
verance (and swimming prowess), but also showed how Harold's
physical courage could lead to recklessness. A woman who grew
up with Lowe in Barmouth was later to claim that he had saved
her brother's life but in the process imperilled his own, although
the exact details of this reported incident are elusive. Locally he was
known to be a smart lad, but his role in another incident of note
indicates that when mischief among the local boys was afoot, Harold
Lowe was a ringleader.

It is recorded that he and a group of comrades took a boat far
enough out to sea in dangerous weather that onlookers ashore feared

they were in danger. The lifeboat *Jones-Gibb* was dispatched to the
rescue. One can well appreciate the trepidation with which the boys
watched the approach of the *Jones-Gibb*. Launching the lifeboat was
no light matter, and when it was ascertained that the boys had occa-
sioned a false alarm they could hardly expect to be popular with
either the lifeboat crew or their own families. As the lifeboat finally
pulled alongside, the insouciant Harold chimed in with the query:
'Where are you bound?' It was a touch of bravado that would later
be the hallmark of many of Harold's recorded remarks regarding an
episode of high drama.

In the October following Harold's misadventure in the punt,
the town was lashed by a southwesterly gale and an unusually high
tide that destroyed extensive sections of the sea walls, made the
Marine Parade impassable, flooded houses, submerged Arthog and
Barmouth Junction railway stations and destroyed fields and fences.
In one stable a horse was found to be swimming in the inrush of sea.
Businesses were shut, telegraphic communication cut off for one
morning and railway traffic almost totally ceased. Barmouth's towns-
people feared for their family members at sea, and there was a rush
of reassuring telegrams when the service was resumed. But when
the weather had finally calmed and the assessment of the damage
began, the receding waters left a sickening surprise. Washed ashore
was the battered, headless body of a man. No identification could be
made; the verdict recorded at the inquest was: 'Found washed ashore
on the beach in the parish of Llanddwywe.' The nameless man was
buried swiftly and quietly.

Harold cultivated other talents in childhood beyond his skill with
boats. The Lowe boys were accomplished singers, an area in which
the Welsh traditionally excel. Members of the Anglican Church,
George Ernest Lowe had belonged to the choir of St David's church,
and his younger brothers Harold and Edgar sang in the choir of the
grand, new St John's church which stood high on the slopes where
the town was built. Harold always took great pleasure in music and
enjoyed singing, and the 'Penrallt Boys', as they were known locally,
performed at small local entertainments and fundraisers.

With George's passing Harold now assumed the role of eldest
son, and with it came certain hopes and expectations. George Lowe
seems to have been determined to give his sons the best education
possible. In November 1897 the two eldest boys, Harold and Edgar,

transferred from the 6th grade of the Barmouth Board School to the newer Barmouth County Intermediate School. By the standards of the day Harold Lowe received a very good education. Prior to the nineteenth century the Welsh education system had lagged behind that of the rest of Britain. It was rare for any child to be educated above the elementary level and in 1881 a departmental committee reported to Gladstone that only 1,540 children in Wales had received any kind of grammar-school education. The intermediate school encouraged bilingualism in the students, and use of Welsh as well as English was practiced. Although his family were Anglo-Welsh rather than native Welsh, Lowe was fluent in the Welsh language.

Although George had plans for his sons that included selecting a career for Harold, the schoolboy had already decided upon his career. For all that he had been exposed to its unforgiving nature, he would follow the sea. Militating against this resolution was his father's determination to apprentice him to a Liverpool firm. It might be conjectured that George Lowe, following the drowning of one son, was keen to instil sterner discipline in those remaining. Headstrong Harold responded by running away from home.

Harold's reasons for fleeing family and Barmouth were given to the world in 1912 at the US Senate inquiry into the *Titanic* disaster:

> My father wanted to apprentice me, but I said I would not be apprenticed; that I was not going to work for anybody for nothing, without any money; that I wanted to be paid for my labour. That was previous to my running away. He took me to Liverpool, to a lot of offices there, and I told him once and for all that I meant what I said. I said 'I am not going to be apprenticed and that settles it.'[4]

There is also another important factor to consider in Harold's dashing away to the sea. Life in the Lowe family, even prior to George Junior's death, was not idyllic. George Lowe – 'Pa' to his children – was, as his grandson phrased it, 'rather fond of the bottle'.[5] What is not known is the extent to which George Lowe's over-imbibing was reflected in his conduct towards those closest to him. He was later described by the residents of Barmouth who knew him as a 'happy drunk', but the face a drinker shows to the world is not necessarily that shown to his own family.

The artist's indulgence in drink led directly to his son forswearing alcohol for his entire life. Possibly George's conduct was unpleasant or even violent enough to warrant his son's abhorrence of alcohol, or perhaps Harold's decision was prompted by his regret at the spectacle of his father squandering his talents and resources on the bottle.

One of Harold's brothers was to follow his father in this predisposition with unhappy consequences for his own children. Whatever his reasons, the end result was the same – Harold Lowe renounced alcohol, objecting even to the description of 'teetotaller': 'I am not a teetotaller, I am a total abstainer.'[6]

When he flatly stated that 'I am not going to be apprenticed, and that settles it', he would prove to be a man – or rather, a boy – of his word.

CHAPTER 2

BOATMAN AND SAILOR

Harold Lowe may have been running away from problems at home – a poor relationship with his father and a career to which he was adamantly opposed – but he was also taking active steps towards a life he had already decided upon. He knew the career he wanted lay with the sea and ocean-going vessels.

Lowe would later claim he was fourteen when he left home, but school records show that he was enrolled at school in late 1897, and it would seem that he was at least fifteen when he took off. The sea provided a ready escape for boys and men from real or imagined problems, or so the popular belief ran, encouraged by a culture of Nelsonic mythology and *Boy's Own* tales.

The reality was somewhat different, as seasoned mariners knew and tried to warn young men seeking adventure. Master mariner Frank Bullen wrote in 1900: 'I have often wished it were possible to make lads who at school chatter so glibly about 'running away to sea', understand how impossible it is to do any such thing nowadays, except, indeed, in such vessels as are the last resort of the unfortunate.'

The only real option for Harold Lowe as a would-be ship's boy was a coaster, one of those that traded in home waters save for short trips across the Channel or to Ireland. Lowe, who came from a small community with a strong seafaring history, was by no means as starry-eyed as an inland boy with no practical experience, but even this background could not have entirely prepared him for the rigours of life at sea.

The first issue to be addressed was finding a ship that would take a slight, wiry teenager. His experience with boats was in his favour, but would not automatically buy his berth. There were also practical considerations – how to get to Portmadoc, the nearest significant port? The train was a possibility, but it is likely that Lowe took the cheapest available option and simply walked.

Griffith Roberts, who ran away to sea in the early 1880s, relates: 'Many a time I ran away from home to try and get a ship to go to sea. Once I walked 15 miles to a village called Portmadoc, and walked back the same day.' He had to take his shoes and socks off and roll up his trouser legs to cross the river to avoid paying the toll gate in two places, the Brewet Bridge and The Cobb. The saving was a penny a time.[7]

By the mid-1890s Portmadoc was just emerging from a prolonged economic depression. These were the last days of the schooners, sometimes picturesquely known as the Western Ocean Yachts. Here a young solicitor's clerk, David Lloyd George, destined to have a major impact on the shipping industry with his later maritime reforms, spent his early days on the slate quays.

The future prime minister well knew the ships, their masters and crews. Along with most of his friends, he had initially wanted to be a seaman. He had heard the stories of voyages to distant ports and storms at sea, young first voyagers proudly displaying their 'bluchers' – the shoes they wore home from Hamburg.

How Lowe found his first berth is not known, but the same word of mouth would have directed him to an agent, many of whom operated out of public houses, whose task it was to match crews to skippers. He might alternatively have directly approached the master of a ship berthed in port. The captain would first examine his hands to see if they were satisfactorily calloused, a process in Lowe's case that would reveal his greenness if he tried to pass himself off as anything more than he was. The often disheartening task of seeking a ship would become very familiar in years to come, but on this first time he eventually found a schooner willing to take him on.

The job of assistant to the ship's cook was often given to boys on their first voyages, a position filled by them with various degrees of competence. Some were grumblingly said to possess the ability to burn salt water. It was likely in this position, at the very bottom of a ship's hierarchy, that Lowe first shipped to sea.

Harold summed up his early career for the United States Inquiry into the *Titanic* disaster:

I ran away and went on these schooners, and from there I went to square-rigged sailing ships, and from there to steam, and got all my certificates, and then I was for five years on the West African Coast in service there, and from there I joined the White Star Line.

This account of his career to 1912, delivered in order to outline his experience, gives little idea of the discipline and application involved in climbing the long hard ladder from ship's boy to master mariner with one of the world's elite passenger lines.

Lowe was rapidly disabused of any romantic notions he had about life before the mast. The work was physically hard and frequently dangerous. Besides the dangers of shipwreck, being swept overboard in high seas, or of a fall from aloft, there were many other real hazards that claimed many lives. In the twenty years to 1899 some 1,153 British ships simply went missing, with the loss of over 11,000 lives.

Lowe was quartered with the rest of the crew in the fo'c'sle (the forecastle, 'before the mast', just behind the ship's bows), in conditions that were both cramped and unsanitary. The men slept in narrow bunks or hammocks, storing their possessions in a sea chest. The heat of summer and the tropics, the icy breath of winter – all permeated the quarters and affected the men within.

The watch system divided each man's day into four hours of work followed by four hours' rest, with two 'dog watches' of two hours each in the afternoon and in the evening. The dog watches, 4–6 p.m. and 6–8 p.m., broke up the sequence so the men did not work the same hours, but had variation.

Lowe learned to live to a day regulated at all hours by the striking of a bell. The first half-hour of the new watch was signified by a single strike of the ship's bell, and two chimes indicated the end of an hour. At the end of a four-hour watch the bell would be struck eight times.

The food aboard ships was of poor quality due to storage problems and parsimonious owners. Portions were meagre and utterly inadequate given the physical needs of the men. Lloyd George of Portmadoc, elected to parliament in 1890, had long been aware of the deficiencies. When appointed president of the Board of Trade in 1906 he shepherded through Parliament a consolidated Merchant Shipping Act aimed at improving the lot of seafarers.

For the first time, a food scale was introduced to regulate the apportionment of victuals, with minimum allotment of basic staples. Lime or lemon juice, the traditional protection against scurvy, was also substantially increased. It also became a requirement that certain ships had to require a certified cook.

While conditions generally took years to improve, the lot of a ship's boy remained a rough one: 'Life on board a Welsh schooner in those days was a particularly hard one, more kicks than ha'pence, especially for the poor boys,' wrote Robert Davis.[8] But as ports of call were mostly close together, Lowe always had the option of jumping ship if his situation became intolerable.

He did not abandon the sea – then or ever. What held him to it? Many a boy had run away to sea, before and since, only to be beaten by the hardship and to return sheepishly to their families. Lowe was always tenacious, a trait that kept him in the fo'c'sle until he fitted into the world of his choice. He also seems to have found in seafaring a niche that suited his rugged individualism and independent streak. No longer was he beholden to his family or his father in particular. He occupied a world where his skills of 'sailorising' made him free to make his own way in life.

Years later Lowe discovered the poetry and writings of Robert Service, whose vision of freedom and 'manliness' would closely reflect his own:

> Since I have seized my own liberty I am a fanatic for freedom. It is now a year ago I launched on my great adventure. I have had hard times, been hungry, cold, weary. I have worked harder than ever I did and discouragement has slapped me on the face. Yet the year has been the happiest of my life.
>
> And all because I am free. By reason of filthy money no one can say to me: Do this, or do that. 'Master' doesn't exist in my vocabulary. I can look any man in the face and tell him to go to the devil. I belong to myself. I am not for sale. It's glorious to feel like that. It sweetens the dry crust and warms the heart in the icy wind. For that I will live austerely and deny myself all pleasure. After health, the best thing in life is freedom.[9]

Apart from hard work and brutal duty, Lowe excelled in the traditional forms of handiwork and took up a lifelong interest in modelling ships. Whether due to nature or nurture, Lowe also exhibited some of his father's artistic flair. He sketched landscapes and ships in pen and pencil. Examples of his work in watercolour also survive, which show an affinity for colour rather than form or perspective. Carving in wood and bone was another hobby that would last Lowe a lifetime once taken up, and some pieces in ivory still exist. He was proud of his work, often appending his name or initials to his creations. Nautical themes predominated, as they do with most scrimshaw or sailors' work.

Another traditional art would leave a permanent mark. Tattooing flourished among British sailors after the first voyage of Captain Cook in 1769, and at some point in his early voyages Lowe decided to adorn himself in the time-honoured way. A heart with his initials appeared on his right forearm, possibly the work of one of his shipmates during a quiet spell off watch.

In smaller vessels the galley was merely a 'caboose', a small cabin on deck, often too small for the cook to get into. He would stand on the deck, clothed in oilskins, with his head in the stifling smoke of the galley, doing his cooking. It was impossible to keep the fire alight in bad weather, and at such times the men subsisted on biscuits and cold water. On one of these early voyages Lowe found himself faced with the frustrating problem of a fire that would not light. With tenacity – and the use of kerosene – he was eventually able to get the fire to draw. It wasn't until later that he found that one of the sails had dropped over the oven flue, with the result that, for a time at least, the ship cut the waves with a black-rimmed hole in the mainsail. The reaction of his crew and skipper went unrecorded.[10]

Details of Lowe's first ships – a total of seven schooners, by his account – remain sketchy. The earliest known was the *Merrion Lass* of Carnarvon, an obscure vessel that does not appear in Lloyd's register although listed in port records. She carried only two or three crewmen, typical of the other ships of this early part of Lowe's career. Some of the seven might more properly have been called be smacks, sloops or ketches. They were the workhorses of the sea, transporting cargoes such as limestone, slate, bricks, tiles or agricultural goods. They often discharged their cargoes on open beaches into waiting farmer's carts that would draw up as close as the ebbing tide allowed, hoping to have the ship unloaded and reloaded in time to catch the next tide.

These early voyages on the *Merrion Lass* and her kind left few extant records, and the first clear record of Lowe's career – the point from which he began documenting his sea-time – comes on 28 May 1900, when he signed on a ship in Portmadoc. She was the *William Keith,* a coasting schooner built at Port Dinorwic, registered in Caernarfon, and owned by Captain Rees Jones of Barmouth. Her age – she had launched in 1859 – testified to the durability of such craft. Only some 99 tons, she carried little more than half a dozen crew including master and mate.

The *William Keith* was of a class of vessel that ferried slate to London, Ireland and further afield – the Elbe, Baltic, Cadiz, Scandinavian and even Newfoundland ports. If the ships didn't return in ballast they might return with timber, lime, cement, potatoes or onions.

Captain Rees Jones typified the Welsh schooner master. He had sailed the world, but now confined himself to Portmadoc and London. Almost sixty years old and suffering from asthma that would kill him in a few years, he was reputedly 'genial' and 'unostentatious'. Between voyages he would return to his wife in Barmouth and indulge his angling hobby.

Lowe, who had moved slightly up the ship's pecking order, could now account himself an ordinary seaman or 'OS.'There was no formal recognised method to make the transition. Much depended on the temperament of the master involved. An OS could stand a trick at the wheel and had a part to play in sail handling and maintenance.

At times an ordinary's position could be hardly more enviable than that of a boy. Frank Bullen wrote of 'such treatment of an O.S. in a ship's fo'c'sle at the hands of men, who certainly did not deserve to wield any authority, as was sufficient to make a lad wish himself dead.' He might find himself compelled to wait for his food until everyone else had been served only to find that half of his allowance had been taken, or forced to be a servant to the other men.The harder edges of Lowe's personality were honed in these years, along with the ability to look out for himself and seize opportunities as they arose.

He served a five-month stint aboard the vessel, travelling in that time to Dublin. The *William Keith*'s crew accounts list him as 'Harry Low'. This version of his surname might have dated to early days when he had run away from home, but as several of his crewmates, including the captain, hailed from the small community of Barmouth it is hard to believe they were unaware that 'Harry' was one of the Lowes of Penrallt. In later years he would object to the diminutive form of his name and be most emphatically 'Harold.'

Lowe signed off the *William Keith* on 30 October 1900, and his next berth does not appear until January of 1901. Gaps appear frequently in his record of service, and may be attributable to several causes. Seamen might spend periods living off their wages, or might have difficulty in finding a new ship. Staying with schooners, he next joined the *British Queen*, registered in Barrow, and remained with her until June of 1901.

The *British Queen*, an iron-hulled vessel, had been built at Preston in 1864 when she was purchased by Thomas Ashcroft of Barrow. In the late 1870s she joined the larger Barrow fleet of James Fisher. She would remain in service until sold by Fisher in 1924, and legend had it that she was the company's last sailing vessel. Like the *William Keith* she was to enjoy remarkable longevity and was finally broken up as late as 1955 at the venerable age of ninety-one.

Lowe struck up a friendship aboard the *British Queen* with a crew-man only a year or two older than he: a Scotsman from Stranraer named Adam Robinson. The two shared a Cardiff shore address at 161 Bute Road, a street crowded with sailors' lodgings. In June 1901 both men signed aboard the *Cortez*, intended for South America. Lowe and Robinson were outward bound for a voyage around perilous Cape Horn to the Chilean nitrate port of Iquique. It was Lowe's first known deep sea voyage.

The *Cortez*, at 2,238 tons, was a considerably larger vessel than those he had worked to date. Built at Southampton in 1886, she was recalled by those who knew her as 'a monster ship… but not a success.' Lowe had by now left long behind the Welsh coasting schooners in which he had learned so much practical seamanship. More importantly, he had attained the position of able-bodied seaman (AB), and was drawing a wage of £3 a month.

Command of the *Cortez* was given to Captain P.J. Hawken, a forty-nine-year-old Padstow man. Her crew documents show many of the men were Welsh, Scottish, English and Irish, but there were also Australians, Germans, Swedes, Danes and Norwegians.

Their destination was a remote and desolate port located north of Valparaiso on a narrow plain between the sea and bluffs. Iquique produced rich deposits of nitrate of soda, a natural fertiliser, which drew European sailing ships. Before the nitrate trade began in the 1830s the port had been an insignificant fishing village, but by 1900 it was a city of well-established broad streets and squares.

It had survived fire, earthquake and even a tidal wave. It had also changed hands in a war between Peru and Chile, to whom it was ceded as a condition of a treaty in 1883. Now sailing ships from all over the world sat in the harbour in their many tiers, loading the nitrates and minerals from the plain of Tarapacá, all shipped to the coast by narrow-gauge railroad.

The *Cortez* arrived in Iquique on 1 October 1901 and joined the rest of the sailing vessels in loading. The nitrate was brought out to the ships in sacks by lighter, and hoisted into the hold by winches. From there the stevedoring of the heavy sacks was overseen by a native Chilean, who would stack them in such a way as to ensure that the cargo could not shift during the homeward voyage.

Over the next few days there was a slow trickle of deserters from the ship, fed up with the rigours of shipboard or seduced by the dubious delights of shore life. Out of a crew of forty-two, no fewer than seven jumped ship – among them Lowe's shipmate and friend Adam Robinson, who left the *Cortez* on 4 October and was noted a deserter. One wonders if he tried to induce Lowe to join him; if he did, he failed.

One apprentice, James Moody – later to be sixth officer of the RMS *Titanic* – wrote scathingly of the Nitrate Coast:

I shan't be sorry to get to sea again as these beastly Chile ports are enough to give one the hump. Lying within shouting distance of the shore and yet never being able to go ashore! All the men went for a liberty day, but as that chiefly consists of getting as tight as they can and generally getting locked up I didn't see the sport so stopped aboard.[11]

Abstainer Lowe would not have seen the sport in excessive drinking either.

Seven substitutes were signed to replace those left behind and on 27 October the *Cortez* began her voyage home. It was a long-standing tradition on the Nitrate Coast that, before breaking moorings, a vessel would cheer each ship in the harbour. One man would be chosen to hail a ship, calling for three cheers for that particular vessel, and the crew would give a full-throated response. The ship cheered must reply, and if she failed to do so received loud groans from surrounding vessels – a strange, reverberating sound, particularly if heard at night, and something of a disgrace that the ship in question would never quite live down.

After this ritual was completed the ship could break her moorings fore and aft, a job that involved backbreaking work in getting up the mooring chains. When completed, the *Cortez* began her homeward voyage, including a summer rounding of the Horn. She arrived in Rotterdam on 3 April 1902, where she discharged most of her remaining crew, the master arranging passage for them, including Lowe, back to the United Kingdom.

On his return to England the young sailor, now a bona fide Cape Horner, took lodgings at 182 Windsor Road, Liverpool. He was no stranger to the great maritime city where his mother, Harriet Quick, had been born and spent her childhood before she had met and married his father. It was also the place where George Lowe had tried to apprentice him several years before.

During the first decade of the twentieth century, fuelled and inspired by the wealth of its merchant shipping industry, with her ships traversing the world's oceans, Liverpool was a city bejewelling herself with landmarks. They included the Liver Building, Mersey Docks and Harbour Company, and the Landing Stage, hub of the city's maritime life.

In 1896 the White Star Line moved their main offices to an impressive new building designed by Richard Norman Shaw, a somewhat improved version of his design for the Metropolitan Police of Scotland Yard in London.

Lowe now cherished hopes of securing a berth as an AB, or perhaps even quartermaster or bosun, with either of the big lines of Cunard and White Star. How good it would be to serve aboard the *Ausonia*, the *Caronia*, the *Oceanic* or the *Baltic*.

Liverpool, like all great ports, offered both entertainment and pitfalls for the young sailor. John Masefield, the poet laureate educated for his own seafaring career in HMS *Conway* anchored in the Mersey, grew to know the seafarers in these last days of sail and wrote about the port in his book *New Chum*. Going ashore one day Masefield saw a ship's crew who had been perhaps a year or more at sea and who were on their way to be paid off. They, like Lowe returning from South America, had 'the indescribable look of high endurance, which used to mark the sailing ship man.' Alongside them were the predatory individuals who exploited them:

> With these men, whose manhood had brought perhaps three thousand tons of cargo half round the world, were the harpies who meant to drug and rob them. These creatures, male and female, hung upon them…One of my companions, who knew a little of seaport life, said: 'They won't have their wages long.' I saw so clearly, what was happening. These men were like children, from being so long away from the land. They had known only manhood and shipmates; now they were ashore among scum and sneakthieves. Nobody seemed to mind. These men had kept and

defended and brought home some merchant's ship, at the risk of their lives; now, they were going to be robbed of their earnings. It was clear to all that they were going to be robbed; it did not seem to matter. People had seen the same thing almost daily.

Little had changed since Charles Dickens had written in 1860 of 'Poor Mercantile Jack', who was 'Ill lodged, ill fed, ill used, hocused, entrapped, anticipated, cleaned out', whose lot was to be 'tempest-tossed until you are drowned!'

While the Sailor's Home and societies for the benefit of seamen combated the vices of the city, there were other drawbacks to the career Lowe had chosen. One of greatest fears to be contended with was the lack of continuous employment, a prospect that faced all seamen from the ship's boy up to the second mate (with the exception of those employed with the premier lines).

Liverpool was close to Lowe's Welsh home. Whatever the root causes of the estrangement with his father, by 1901 Harold and George Lowe had managed to patch up their differences to the extent that Harold was using Penrallt as his permanent shore address.

For a month he lived on the £25.1.2 balance of wages he received from the *Cortez*, but if he was holding out for another AB's position he was to be disappointed. On 20 May 1902, he had to sign on the *Balasore*, a four-masted steel barque of 2,561 tons.

Accepting work on the *Balasore* resulted in a drop in pay and position and Lowe was back as an OS at a wage of £2.10.0 per month. The *Balasore* made a virtue of austerity – a handwritten notation in her articles states that there was to be 'no gambling or card playing allowed on Sunday'. Infringements incurred a fine of 10s for each offence.

She sailed on 22 May for Cape Town, arriving at her destination in December. Lowe's month ashore and relocation to Liverpool seem to have left him in need of funds – uncharacteristically, he had to seek an advance on his wages of £1.10.0 after leaving Liverpool. The voyage terminated in Antwerp on 27 January 1903 and Lowe was discharged home the following day.

Next came the *Ormsary*, a four-masted barque. Lowe joined her in March 1903, once more as an AB receiving £3.0.0 monthly. He had been marshalling his resources carefully, and he was now one of the few seamen who did not require an advance on his wages at the time of signing the agreements. The *Ormsary* was a new vessel, launched in

January 1903, and Lowe was to take part in her maiden voyage. She sailed out of Liverpool, bound for Australia, on 14 March.

In June 1903, during the antipodean midwinter, the *Ormsary* sailed between the heads at Sydney Harbour and up past Fort Denison and Bennelong Point to berth in the busy port. This was Lowe's introduction to the great southern continent and Sydney's Port Jackson. For Lowe, like many seamen before and since, the warmth of the inhabitants was to endear Australia to him. This was sufficient inducement for many visiting seamen to jump ship when the opportunity arose, and one of these was the *Ormsary*'s young second mate.

After a month in Sydney the ship moved up the New South Wales coast to Newcastle before departing in mid-August for Honolulu, where she had a three-week stay in October 1903. Then it was back to Sydney, arriving on 12 December. Lowe spent Christmas 1903 in the heat of an Australian summer, with the screeching parrots, thrumming cicadas and heady scent of the eucalyptus forests that dominated the foreshores of Port Jackson. The ship remained until 22 January 1904, then made for home.

The return crossing was not without incident. The *Ormsary* hit heavy weather and on 7 March an eighteen-year-old apprentice, Frederick John Marsh, was lost overboard, casting a gloom over the rest of the voyage. The *Ormsary* at last arrived in Rotterdam and Lowe signed off her articles on 27 May. His fourteen months aboard her had been his longest period with a single vessel to date, and she would prove to be his last ship before entering steam – perhaps the long voyage had finally convinced him to turn to the future of his profession.

It was as well he did, as the *Ormsary* was to meet a strange fate. On 13 September 1906 she sailed from Caleta Coloso with a cargo of nitrate for Antwerp and disappeared without a trace. When all hope had been lost for the missing vessel, *The Shipping Gazette Summary* in May 1907 suggested that the *Ormsary* had probably struck an iceberg in the seas around Cape Horn. In the days before all ships were fitted with wireless such disappearances were not uncommon. She was the fourth vessel posted missing that year, assumed lost amid the southern ice.

CHAPTER 3

IN LINE OF RESERVE

At some time while back in England between these voyages, Harold Lowe had joined the Royal Navy Reserve (RNR). Records for this period are incomplete but his Board of Trade papers show he was 'on drill' for a period between 27 May and 6 August 1904, having been assigned the RNR number 13213. The Royal Navy Reserve went back as far as the French Revolutionary Wars, although the first provision for naval reserves came in 1852, with the provisionally named Royal Naval Volunteers coming into being several years later, and the formation of an officers' reserve in 1861.

Lowe joined the RNR shortly before Admiral Sir John Fisher's abortive attempt to disband it in 1905 resulted instead in its reform into a more effective fighting unit. War with an expansionist Germany was becoming widely expected and the cry of 'two keels for one' had been taken up by campaigning journalist W.T. Stead, later to die on the RMS *Titanic*.

From his formative years at sea the spare-framed seaman Lowe had grown to manhood, attaining a full height of 5ft 8in. His hair still curled in a rather unruly, boyish manner, and he would either crop it or turn to oils and creams, as was the fashion, to bring it under control.

His official description in Board of Trade documents described him as 'dark complexioned' – probably sun-bronzed – and his almond-shaped eyes as 'dark brown'. One admirer would later describe his 'clear cut' features and 'keen, deep set, merry black eyes.' Although generally of a fairly slender and sinewy build, his solid jaw gave substance to his face. Even so, for most of his life he looked younger than his age.

Lowe had a breezy way of talking and tended to gesture with his hands when he spoke. He had a striking knack for a memorable phrase, later to give rise to some of the most famous word pictures associated with the *Titanic* disaster. At the same time, his written words could have an awkward stiltedness to them, as can be seen in some surviving letters.

'Harry Low' had also changed how he himself liked to be addressed. Although in later life he was always known as Harold, around this time he clearly preferred the use of Godfrey, which was his middle name.

A postcard written in 1912 to his fiancée Ellen Whitehouse has Godfrey as the signature, as does a signed and dated family photo from 1914. It was presumably for this reason that a list of survivors of the *Titanic* disaster compiled by the most senior living officer, Second Mate Charles Lightoller, notes him down as 'G. Lowe'.

We have little direct information about Lowe's personal life and development in the intervening years from 1904 to 1912. He was neither a diary-keeper nor a prolific letter-writer. It is possible to draw upon his general circumstances, however, and note for example that as he grew to adulthood his sexuality developed in an environment not always conducive to healthy maturation. The promiscuity of sailors is firmly entrenched in popular myth but such appetites arise more from the limitations of their profession than from any innate rapacity.

The very nature of the occupation, with long periods of forced same-sex company and limited opportunities for physical intimacy with women, led inevitably to bouts of indulgence when the chance arose. It was a similar story with alcohol; for some men, either or both were to be partaken to the full when the chance was there.

Sailor towns offered easily accessible sex to sate every desire, with predictable results. Gonorrhoea and syphilis, the 'pox' and the 'clap', were all rife and feared, with treatment consisting of essentially poisoning the sufferer with substances such as mercury in a bid to contain the disease. Men risked sterility and even their sanity and lives for meagre comfort or a bit of pleasure. Although the medical expenses of seamen were supposed to be borne by the shipowners under the 1906 Merchant Shipping Act, venereal disease was specifically excluded from its provisions. It was only after the final report of the British Royal Commission into Venereal Diseases in 1916 that there were widespread efforts at education and free treatment in clinics. Measures were being developed to tackle a problem so rife in the Navy and Merchant Marine, but understanding of the diseases themselves was still evolving. The infection (*treponema pallidum*) responsible for syphilis was only identified in 1905, which was

followed by the development of the Wasserman test in 1906 that
made diagnosis easier. Effective treatment had to wait until the discovery of Salvarsan in 1910.

It might be asked if Lowe indulged in the quayside prostitutes.
The question cannot be answered with certainty. Accounts of wages
for his ships suggest he was not spending much money at all on
shoreside entertainment of any description. Lowe could exhibit tremendous self-discipline if he needed to and some men did remain
celibate in spite of peer pressure and the opportunities that surrounded them when in port. If he did exercise his needs in this
time-honoured manner he was discreet or lucky, and was eventually
to father two healthy children in a happy marriage.

Venereal disease was of course not the only factor making seafaring
a risky line of work. The range of risks sailors faced in their daily
duty was commented upon by a 1908 parliamentary committee on
dangerous trades. Seamen suffered mortality rates in every age group
far in excess of shore-based males. In the fifteen to thirty-five age
group the rate was more than double the norm.

Alcoholism, diseases of the liver, cancer, tuberculosis, Bright's disease and ailments of the nervous, circulatory and respiratory systems
were particularly highlighted. But the potential for loss of life from
accident was monumental – four and a half times the average for
other male workers.

His RNR training stint done, Lowe's next two ships brought him
into contact with one of the world's premier shipping companies,
the Blue Funnel Line. Although these voyages took just over a year
in total, they would leave a marked impression on Lowe as he travelled throughout the Near and Far East, and all the way to Japan.

AB Harold Lowe initially signed aboard the *Prometheus*, running
to the Orient. The *Prometheus*, 5,000 tons and 400ft in length, thus
became his first steamer. He would never go back to sail.

The transition to steam was a necessity for an ambitious young
seaman who wanted to get on in his profession. But it still represented something of an upheaval for individuals trained and
employed in sail. James Moody, destined to join Lowe as an officer
on the decks of the *Titanic*, joined his first steamer in 1908 and
described it as a voyage in 'a hot water bottle'. He went on to express
the anxieties of many: 'I am very nervous starting this job, as there
are millions of things I don't know on a steamer and I never open
my mouth without I shall have my foot in it, as they say!'[12]

Another *Titanic* officer, Charles Lightoller, felt a pang of regret for leaving behind 'the towering tiers of bellying canvas, the sound of the water rushing past the scupper holes' and the 'feel of something living under my feet', but for career advancement the unsentimental switch had to be made.[13] Old salts may have sneered about 'leaving the sea and going into steam', but there was no doubt that the food was better and the voyages far more predictable. The debit side included a constant throbbing of machinery and the grime of coaling.

After calling at Java on the return leg of her voyage, the *Prometheus* was involved in an incident in Amsterdam that would bring about Lowe's first brush with Board of Trade legal proceedings.

On 10 November 1904, while proceeding up a canal from the sea, she encountered the larger *Pectan*, a vessel of 7,291 tons and approximately 500ft long, heading seaward in ballast on her way to Texas. Both ships were under pilotage and were due to pass red-to-red, or port side to port side.

The *Pectan*, anticipating difficulties with a manoeuvre involving two large vessels in such close proximity, reversed her engines with the result that she canted to starboard and touched the bank on the northern side of the canal. She blew three short blasts on her whistle, but the *Prometheus*'s port side came into contact with the quarter of the *Pectan* and caused the larger ship damage.

There would be a sequel. The *Prometheus* discharged in Amsterdam and returned to Liverpool, where the crew signed off on Lowe's twenty-second birthday, 21 November 1904. On 1 March 1905 the Board of Trade Inquiry opened.

As the plaintiffs presented their case, it was described how the *Pectan,* passing a point where the canal was crossed by a footbridge, sighted the *Prometheus* underneath a railway bridge 800 yards away. After running aground in her efforts to avoid difficulties with the *Prometheus*, she attempted twice to signal the Alfred Holt ship. The *Prometheus*, however, although in a position to ascertain that the *Pectan* was in difficulties, continued to approach – allegedly causing the collision.

The *Prometheus* argued that both ships were proceeding on their respective sides of the canal and it was believed there would be no difficulty in the ships slipping past each other. When the *Pectan* was quite close she had suddenly sheered across the canal and her stern swung down upon the *Prometheus*. Although the latter attempted to reverse engines at the last moment it was too late to avoid impact.

In summing up the case the president pointed to some discrep-
ancies in evidence, both in documents and testimony. In the main,
though, he accepted the *Pectan*'s case that the *Prometheus* had time to
ascertain and respond to the difficulties *Pectan* was experiencing and
did not do so. Witnesses from the footbridge and the tug attending
Pectan provided corroborative evidence for the larger ship's case, and
the *Prometheus* was found solely responsible.[14]

It was Lowe's first experience with providing witness testimony
at a trial or inquiry. Such proceedings were viewed with suspicion
by seamen, although there is no reason in this instance to suspect
that the judgement was anything but a fair one. Lowe would meet
two of the lawyers involved, Aspinall and Laing, during the 1912
inquiry into the loss of the *Titanic*. Lowe's evidence does not survive, but it may be that he toed the company line and presented his
evidence in a light that owed more to loyalty to Blue Funnel than
to strict veracity. He would later prove himself not so much a company man as something of a maverick, perhaps having been soured
by the *Prometheus* experience. As Board of Trade proceedings went,
however, it was a fairly minor affair and all parties were keen to see it
settled with a minimum of fuss.

He was soon back at sea, joining the *Telemachus* under the command of Captain J.H. Goodwin. In addition to thirteen Europeans,
she also carried a Chinese crew, signed on under separate agree-
ment. Blue Funnel had pioneered the use of Chinese crews aboard
their ships, to tremendous success. Many of these old sailors would
eventually settle in Liverpool, forming part of the thriving Chinese
community in that port.

There was, however, a good deal of friction between the
European and Asian crewmen. Fear for their employment and
wages on the part of the British crew could easily manifest itself as
bigotry. It had been something of a struggle before the rights of the
Chinese crew to be a part of the British Mercantile Marine were
acknowledged at all.

Lowe, who would be accused of racism for remarks made at the
Titanic Inquiry, had no objections to working with a Chinese crew.
Those Chinese he sailed with on these Alfred Holt voyages left him
with a positive impression. Contrary to the concept of a supposedly
'devious' Oriental race, already a widely held stereotype, those who
sailed with him in the Blue Funnel ships were, in his experience,
both honest and hard working, traits he strongly respected.

A story from this period featured a man described in accounts as a 'Chinaman' falling overboard. Lowe, who was already on the ship's sick list suffering from blood poisoning in his arm, jumped after the unfortunate man without hesitation, and held him above water until assistance could be dispatched for them both.[15]

The *Telemachus* reached Colombo, Ceylon, at the end of March. After a brief stop at Singapore, April found her in the Japanese ports of Kobe and Nagasaki. In early May 1905 she crossed the Pacific to reach Vancouver on 22 May. It was Lowe's first visit to the United States. The vessel steamed along the Pacific North-West shores to Seattle and Tacoma, before turning once again for Japan and then on to Shanghai, Hong Kong and Southeast Asian ports. She called at Jeddah, then sailed through the Suez Canal before touching at Marseilles and Amsterdam, before finally reaching Liverpool. It was October before the crew were signed off.

Another anecdote may also relate to this period, as it concerns a vessel returning from Japan, although it may pertain to an earlier period in sail. In the midst of a 'terrific gale' the captain called out for a volunteer to climb the rigging and perform an unspecified task essential to the ship's safety. There were no takers among the crew. Finally Lowe's response was: 'I will go, I may as well die from the yard as the deck.'[16]

He was already establishing a reputation for feats of physical courage when circumstances demanded. The Barmouth boy who had led local lads into mischief had developed an ability to take quick, decisive action.

Lowe was by now nurturing his latent ambition. He had aspirations beyond the fo'c'sle, and was looking towards certification as a ship's officer. He would be in competition with those who had served four-year apprenticeships which, in theory, were to equip them with the necessary skills for the first piece of coveted paperwork, that of second mate.

It was said of those who had come to their position as an officer via the fo'c'sle rather than the quarterdeck that they had 'come up through the hawse pipe', and this was the route Lowe would follow. He might not have had the advantages a formal apprenticeship could offer, but he acquired the necessary textbooks and applied himself with single-minded determination. After signing off from the *Telemachus* Lowe settled down to study in earnest for his examinations.

He sat for second mate in January 1906. He was twenty-three, the age when most who had come through the apprenticeship system were applying for their full master's ticket. But Lowe's first attempt at the exam was unsuccessful, and he failed 'Rules of the Road'. Frustrated, he had to do six months' more sea time before he could sit the examination again.

Such failures were far from exceptional – Lightoller explained that it was not uncommon to fail three or four times for one ticket, and he even knew a case of a man who made seven attempts at achieving a master's certification. Lowe swallowed whatever injuries his pride received and returned to sea.

Those six months saw him serve with the ships of the Ellerman line, first with the *Justin*, and then the *Fabian*. The latter departed Liverpool on 29 May 1906, bound for Alexandria and other Mediterranean ports. When the voyage was completed in July he stayed ashore at Liverpool to re-apply for his Second Mate's certificate. He took the test for the second time on 20 August. This time he passed.

For many young men, seafaring was a family tradition. On the *Titanic*'s bridge, Captain Smith and officers Lightoller, Murdoch and Boxhall all had relatives who made their living on the seas. This, of course, had its advantages. 'What, then, is the young newly passed officer to do when, with his creamy new certificate in his pocket, he finds nothing before him in his old firm but a voyage before the mast as an able seaman?' asked Frank Bullen in *Men of the Merchant Service*.

> Well, if his folks have any acquaintances among shipowners – in other words, any influence in that direction – now is the time to use it. Or, if they have money to invest, they will not find it difficult to purchase a certain amount of interest which, should, and generally does, result in their son getting an opening for employment. But if neither of these levers are available, the aspirant is almost certainly in for a bad time.

There was already a glut of merchant marine officers, and Lowe was without leverage or any form of patronage. There was no guarantee that he would find work in the capacity of his new qualification. In his position, so young men were advised, he might find it necessary to put aside his pride and take up work as an AB again until he could find berth as an officer.

CHAPTER 4

'A GOOD BRIDGE OFFICER'

Lowe was on the eve of his twenty-fourth birthday, and he had spent some nine years at sea, with extensive experience both in sail and steam. He needed luck to find a ship willing to sign him on as an officer. It meant being in the right place at the right time, rising early and trudging the rounds of the shipping offices and keeping his ear to the ground for opportunities as they arose. Unwilling to ship back to sea as an AB, he held out for a third mate's position, and by October his funds were running very low. Finally he found the SS *Ardeola*, a vessel of 1,384 gross tons, whose third mate had abruptly left.

As third mate, he was at the beck and call of more senior officers. In the days of sail most ships carried only the captain and a first and second mate, but the increasing size of ships had brought about a more complex structure of governance. The number of mates – or officers, as they were increasingly being termed – varied from vessel to vessel, up to master and seven deck officers on some of the larger Atlantic liners.

This first voyage as a ship's officer took him to him to the Canary Islands, where the *Ardeola* loaded fruit. The voyage was a comparatively brief one and Captain Maclean gave him a reference noting that he was an 'attentive officer to his various duties, always obliging and strictly sober.' He must have been pleased indeed when a position next arose with one of the most prominent lines. For some decades the Elder Dempster ships with their buff funnels had dominated the West African runs. Lowe joined the *Chama* as fourth mate.

Steamers serving Africa often had to navigate river deltas and estuaries best suited for dug-out canoes or paddleboats. Bumping over sandbars and running into banks and soft mud bottoms wasn't uncommon. In some mangrove swamp areas the channel was so narrow that the only way to navigate a sharp bend was to drive the bow into the bank and wait for the tide to swing the ship's stern. Dredging was unheard of, and facilities were primitive.

Cargo was often handled at 'surf ports', requiring 'surf boats' which the officers and crew had to load or unload. In addition to the heat there were other perils to face, most notably disease-carrying mosquitoes. Malaria was a killer, and the only means of combating it was quinine.

Charles Lightoller, who would later serve with Lowe on the *Titanic*, also spent some years with Elder Dempster back in the 1890s. In one instance he was the only survivor of a capsized surf boat, an incident triggered by a bullying master who had provoked him into attempting to land in pounding waves at Grand Bassam. Malaria proved the final straw for Lightoller, who gave up the African coast after contracting the disease.

There were no pilots, and ships relied on the experience of their captains and officers. Lowe developed new skills in navigating the uncharted waters. One technique was to observe the course of the ebb tide, which usually indicated the deepest channel.

Captain George Hough of the *Chama* was pleased with Lowe's performance and thought him 'a good young officer'. The line itself was satisfied enough to bump him up from fourth to third mate, and Lowe served in that capacity on the first of several journeys aboard the *Bonny*, home ported in Hamburg.

It was probably while aboard her that he discovered one of the perks of the West African run. Many a Jack Tar had brought back a parrot, monkey or other creature to serve as a novel form of company at sea with the added incentive of earning a bit of money through eventual disposal at home. Lowe, who had a lifelong affinity with animals, found that collecting African wildlife for sale in Europe was one way in which a junior officer could supplement his income. He transported specimens for Germany's Hagenbeck Zoo in his own cabin, leading to one incident with a large primate that he would later recount with humour as resembling a boxing match.

If animals were a form of live cargo, people were another. Now that Lowe was an officer he was brought into frequent contact with passengers. They were certainly more difficult to deal with than the goods and livestock with which Lowe was more accustomed. 'They could not be stowed in the holds under battened hatches, and forgotten. They were free to roam at random within their class accommodation' wrote one contemporary.

An officer off watch could not spend all his time in his cabin and or the mess and it was inevitable that he would come into contact with curious passengers who assumed that authority and knowledge went with the uniform: "'What makes the sea blue?"; "Where do seagulls sleep?"; "What speed are we doing?"; "What causes fog?"; "Will we see any icebergs?"; "What causes the Gulf Stream?"; or, as the quizzer points to a wisp of smoke on the horizon, "What ship is that?" – these are only specimen openings in the game of "Ask the Officer (he knows)."'[17]

Between voyages Lowe lodged at 7 College View in Bootle, a Liverpool suburb bordering the docks, known as 'Brutal Bootle'. Lightoller wrote in *Titanic and Other Ships* of the firemen who resided there: 'A tougher bunch on a Western Ocean Mail boat it would be impossible to find. Bootle seemed to specialize in Liverpool Irishmen, who were accounted the toughest of the tough.'

The shore accommodation was nonetheless to Lowe's taste. The terraced digs were at the end of a short street that also housed the public baths, an impressive Victorian edifice of sandstone and elaborate carving. But he had had enough of water for the time being. Instead Lowe would rise early and spend the morning hours pacing the garden, textbook in hand, studying the material he was required to master. It was not enough to have experience at sea, for evidence of understanding had to be presented in a format demanded by the examiners, a challenge that could defeat even the saltiest of seamen.

On 20 July 1908, Lowe sat for his First Mate's certificate at Liverpool. As with his first attempt for Second, he failed at the first try, tripped up by navigational questions. Just over a week later he sat the exam again – this time passing. He returned to Elder Dempster, joining the crew of the *Madeira* that September, now very much a second mate. Further promotion came during the voyage, when he was called upon to serve in the giddy heights of chief officer.

In December Lowe joined the *Oron*. The new ship promised more comfort as she was fitted with electric lights and refrigeration, unlike the *Madeira,* and had 'plenty of salt beef carried in casks of brine,' and 'two pigs for fattening up during the voyage.'[18]

Suddenly tragedy struck at home. On 21 March 1909, Lowe's mother Harriet fell ill at her son Arthur's home in Fairbourne. 'Apoplexy' – the term used for paralysis caused by a stroke, the same condition that had felled her father – was given as the cause. She quickly lapsed into a coma and died.

How close Lowe had been to the woman who had given him birth is unknown. Most sources only refer to his colourful father. She does seem to have been a hugely practical and efficient woman,

as after her children left home, Harriet ran Penrallt, the house on
the slope, as a private hotel. While George lapsed from brush to
bottle and back again, Lowe's mother determinedly advertised her
'very high class' establishment, with 'secluded gardens', superb views
and 'excellent cuisine'. Perhaps Harriet was indeed the source of
Lowe's iron will and ferocious dedication, characteristics notably
absent in his father, but in any case she was soon swallowed up in the
anonymity of death, aged only fifty-three.

Harold may have made it home from West Africa for the funeral.
The dates for his service show a gap around the time when his
mother's coffin was carried up to Llanaber churchyard where her
eldest son George already lay. The headstone that Harold had erected
over the grave many years later gives an incorrect date of death.

Lowe returned to sea in the middle of 1909. He signed aboard the
Addah, and did four voyages with her, each lasting almost exactly four
months. The ability to keep so precisely to schedules was one of the
advantages of steam. She was nearly identical to her sister, the *Chama*,
in which Lowe had previously served. One of the *Addah*'s voyages illustrated the perils associated with the West African trade. On
22 September she sailed from Liverpool for Tenerife, arriving there
six days later. She then made her way to Dakar, and began calling at
the usual ports – Rufesque, Bathurst, Sierra Leone and Grand Bassam.

In November a twenty-five-year-old crewman named Weiss
reported that he had been feeling unwell for some days. Examined by
the ship's surgeon, gaunt-cheeked Patrick Black, he was diagnosed as
suffering from malaria. All medical assistance was rendered, but there
was little to be done beyond the administration of quinine. Weiss
continued to weaken and was soon fighting for his life. Meanwhile a
muster of passengers and crew revealed that one of the kroo labourers,
referred to only as 'Freeman', appeared to be suffering from what Dr
Black suspected was smallpox. He was immediately isolated, and on
the following day the tentative diagnosis was devastatingly confirmed.

It was with good reason that those who travelled to Africa feared
smallpox. The virus is highly communicable and carried a 30 per
cent fatality rate. Those lucky enough to survive bore its disfiguring
effects as lifelong scars.

The ship was put immediately into quarantine, with Freeman in
isolation. Weiss, meanwhile, was rapidly deteriorating. At 3 a.m. on
2 December, a few hours after the *Addah* left Cape Palmas, Captain
Hough ordered that he be moved to a saloon cabin where he might

be made more comfortable. But an hour and a half after being moved, with Black and Hough present, Weiss gave up his spirit.

He was buried at sea the next day with usual rites as a palpable fear began to stalk the ship's complement. Wages of £4.8.10 and a few meagre possessions were carefully inventoried and would later be sent to his family in Hamburg. Weiss was the same age as Harold Lowe, and his death was a stark warning of what could happen to any of them. Lowe contracted malaria himself, and the condition was to recur in his last years before finally being a factor in his own death.

On 4 December the ship arrived in Sierra Leone and was again placed in quarantine. All the kroo labour, including Freeman, were landed under the supervision of the port authorities. The ship was then thoroughly disinfected. She remained there for another two days before commencing the homeward voyage, landing at Liverpool three days before Christmas.

A photograph of the senior crew of the *Addah*, in rows of bristling moustaches, white trousers and navy jackets (see picture section, illustration No.4), gives a vivid impression of Second Officer Lowe on the eve of sitting for his master's certification. The other men – deck crew, purser, stewards and surgeon – pose casually in wicker chairs, flanked by life rings. Lowe, standing in the back row, strikes by contrast an almost exaggerated figure. He had developed the habit of wearing his cap at a rakish angle, an affectation popular among junior officers, and in this photo it sits tilted forward over his eyes. The whole effect is somewhat dramatic and Lowe exhibited a propensity for the theatrical throughout his life. Such swagger confidence continued to propel him forward, and from the *Addah* he took the next step in his career.

Knowing he was going up for his examination, Captain Hough, under whom Lowe had served for over a year, was pleased to provide him with a strong reference that drew particular attention to Lowe's abilities as 'a good bridge officer.'[19] On 26 October 1910, Lowe presented himself at the Board of Trade's Liverpool offices for his exam. As with his previous certifications, he yet again failed at the first attempt, becoming unstuck in 'Navigation (ships' business)'. Once more he swiftly re-sat, passing for master less than two weeks later on 7 November.

He would do one more voyage with Elder Dempster, aboard the SS *Zaria*. Arriving back in Liverpool in March 1911, armed with his qualifications and references that included a final testimonial from the *Zaria*'s captain, he applied to the White Star Line.

CHAPTER 5

WHITE STAR LINE

In April 1912, Harold Lowe somewhat inaccurately told the US *Titanic* Inquiry that he had served with the White Star Line for about fifteen months. Charles Bartlett, White Star's Liverpool marine superintendent, corrected him to say that at the time of the disaster Lowe had been with the company for a year.

Lowe's service with Elder Dempster had made him an attractive prospect for the shipping line. The first order of business, however, was a cut in pay – Lowe would have to sacrifice wages for prestige, dropping from the £9 10s he had received as second mate of the *Zaria* to a monthly salary of one pound less the moment he signed on his first White Star ship.

There were personal matters to consider as well as his career. Lowe, now approaching thirty, was attaining as much stability in his life as could be expected of a seafarer. He was also romantically involved with his distant relation, Ellen (Nellie) Marion Whitehouse. Just prior to his joining the White Star Line, the two became engaged.

Nellie's father, William, was the son of clergyman George Lowe Whitehouse. Her mother Rebecca was also the offspring of clergy, in her case the Vicar of Langley. Her parents married in 1884, moving to Wales where Nellie was born on 16 April 1885.

During her childhood the family moved again, to Colwyn Bay, and were still living there when Harold Lowe began his courtship. The immediate past had been difficult for Nellie and her family. Her younger brother, Harold William, fell from a trap in January 1908 and was run over, suffering spinal damage. Harold William, formerly a keen sportsman full of energy and activity, was thrown into a slough of depression by his injuries. His physician recommended a change of scenery, and Harold was dispatched to the Lake District to recover.

After his return home, Harold told his family one day that he was going to post a letter and limped out into the July evening. The Whitehouses were glad he was finally shaking off the emotional

malaise that had afflicted him since his fall. They were still uncon-
cerned when he had not returned by 10.30 p.m., since his movements
were slower now, or perhaps he had gone to visit a friend. By 11 p.m.
they were anxious and began to search the grounds. Nellie went to
the stables and found the door locked. Always perceptive, she knew
something terrible had happened. Finding her parents she anxiously
advised them about the locked door. 'Do not go there' she begged.
'It is better to go for the sergeant'. William Whitehouse, refusing
to accept that anything could be seriously amiss, rushed to force a
window open and entered the stable.

'There I found my son,' Whitehouse told the ensuing inquest.
'God only knows what a shock it gave me to see my only son there,
and only by God's grace can I stand it. It must have been the last
wish upon that poor lad's mind to give you any trouble.' [20]

Harold lay on his back, his clothing saturated with blood, near
him a double-barrel shotgun he had been cleaning earlier in the day.
He had used his laces to attach the rifle to a ladder and fire it. The
twenty-one-year-old had blown away the top half of his skull.

The inquest reached the customary verdict that he had acted while
'of unsound mind' and a vote of condolence was passed. This devastating event coincided with the deepening of Nellie and Harold Lowe's
relationship, and undoubtedly brought the two closer together.

Nellie was a full-figured woman with a sweet smile and Lowe
himself was an attractive prospect for a young woman. The practical young officer was establishing himself well in his career. Breaks
between voyages afforded him the opportunity to visit her in
Colwyn Bay, and the pair eventually reached some sort of 'understanding', as one did in an Edwardian courtship.

It was a solid relationship based on respect and friendship rather
than torrid impulses. Many of Lowe's merchant marine colleagues
met their spouses aboard ship, and romances were common in
spite of company regulations on crew and passenger interaction.
But Nellie was no exotic from a foreign land. The relationship was
entirely conventional. She was essentially someone of the same
Anglo-Welsh background as his own. Her family was also well off
and few sailors would object to a financially secure spouse, given
their own uncertainty of employment. Nellie was a fixed point in an
ever-changing sea, and he treasured a gold-framed miniature of his
fiancée with her calm, anchoring smile.

The White Star Line was not prepared to offer their new recruit one of the front-rank ships. In April 1911, a year before the *Titanic* disaster, a berth was assigned to Lowe on the *Tropic*, a fifteen-year-old modest steamer (8,262 tons) with much to be modest about. It was engaged in the meat trade to Australia. Lowe, twenty-eight years old and with responsibilities to think about, signed on as fourth officer on a monthly wage of £8.

While the *Tropic* was far from the most glamorous vessel in the White Star Line fleet, joining her was an undoubted step up. In an age when there was a surfeit of qualified officers, the major lines could afford to be selective when choosing who went on the bridge of their ships. Lowe would take life-long pride in his White Star service, emblematic of which was the serviette ring he crafted from ivory, embellished with a painted White Star swallowtail flag. On the back he put his name and Penrallt address.

At 9 a.m. on sailing day, 22 April, word was received on the *Tropic* that there was to be a last-minute change in the senior line-up. Third Officer Billiald was transferred, and Fourth Officer Lowe received an instant promotion, moving up to take his place. A substitute signed for both the fourth officer and for an assistant cook who failed to join, a search was made for stowaways, and the *Tropic* cast off for Port Adelaide.

There were minor incidents to relieve the monotony at sea – a few days out of Liverpool a man named John Hagan was discovered in the forward stokehold, having stowed away in a coalbunker. He was put to work on deck. More worryingly, one of the firemen, John Moore, came down with a bad cold that developed into pleurisy. Although the *Tropic* had a crew of sixty-eight, including three livestock handlers, she carried no doctor.

Captain Crossland had to administer aid according to the instructions in a medical guide issued to ships' masters. A seaman was assigned to watch over the invalid, but Moore's temperature soared to 103. He died in Adelaide Hospital on 20 June.

Lowe's duties aboard the *Tropic* were much the same as with previous steamers, except that White Star expected everything to be done to absolute perfection. Charles Lightoller recorded his first impressions of life aboard a White Star Line vessel. 'Here everything was spotless and clean; everything just-so, discipline strict but in no way irksome. Navigation such as I had never known it.'

Leaving Adelaide on 10 June, the *Tropic* steamed to Melbourne, Sydney and Brisbane in turn, all familiar to Lowe from his voyage on the *Ormsary*. She then turned for home, loaded with cattle, calling at Durban and London before arriving back in Liverpool in September 1911.

Lowe's performance on the *Tropic* evidently proved satisfactory, as his next assignment, only days after returning to Liverpool, was to the *Belgic*. She was a 10,000-ton steamer on the Australian route, with a capacity for nearly 2,000 passengers, and would be packed with emigrants on this voyage. A different class of cattle boat entirely.

Newspapers of the time noted that this was the *Belgic's* first voyage to Australia, and carried the first large batch of nominated emigrants. The nominators gave guarantees that employment would be awaiting their nominees and the emigrants were screened before departure.

The vessel left Liverpool with 1,746 souls on board, including a crew of 210. *Belgic* carried five deck officers ranging from chief to fourth – Lowe was third - serving under Captain J.H.Thornton. By the time she arrived in Cape Town on 18 October, there was already trouble simmering aboard among both passengers and crew. Some of the emigrants were of the opinion that the food offered on board was almost unfit for consumption – the meat at times 'began to walk', one man claimed. A young London lady said the meat was sometimes edible, but had been badly preserved and cooked, and some was tainted. She spent most of the voyage in her cabin, she told reporters in Adelaide, and 'when anything was given to us good it had what we called the *Belgic* taint about it. The condition of the boat throughout was simply horrible and I wonder how we all survived the ordeal.' Passengers gossiped that the crew were refusing work, demanding better food than was given to the passengers. The lavatories were also a source of complaint, with charges that they were unclean and unfit for use.

To Captain Thornton's disgust, the conditions on board the *Belgic,* particularly the food, were the subject of a scathing newspaper article when the vessel arrived in Cape Town. He made light of the criticisms when the vessel reached Australia, stating: 'They appeared in a paper that had just been established, and probably the chap who wrote the report had the stomach-ache.'[21]

More than poor food was a cause for concern. Fireman James Sullivan was hauled up before the bench in Cape Town and convicted of assaulting the ship's chief engineer. He was to have been left ashore in jail, but due to an error on the part of the local police, he was returned to the ship with another group of crewmen sentenced to spells in jail for desertion.

Sullivan was not the only firebrand on board, and by the time the vessel reached Fremantle in Western Australia, five or six malcontents had spread such discontent that, according to Captain Thornton, virtually every crewman on board had developed a grievance. The chief cause of the disturbance was a strict enforcement of the rules separating crew and passengers, as some of the crew had been fraternising with the nearly 600 emigrants on board who were bound for the eastern states of Australia.

Members of the crew, resenting the restrictions placed on their consorting with the passengers, attempted to enlist the sympathies of the emigrants. They began to circulate rumours that the vessel was unsafe, claiming she had been drawing a foot more water than when she left Cape Town, and making alarmist claims that the ship would never cross the Great Australian Bight. Firemen, stokers and seamen slipped away ashore. It was also alleged that the captain had told a customs officer in Cape Town that he had 'the scum of Europe aboard', an inflammatory remark that was repeated by the crew in order to bring the emigrants' opinion in line with their own.[22]

As the vessel prepared to sail on the evening of 10 November, an extraordinary scene played out on the Victoria Quay where the *Belgic* was moored. The chief officer approached Captain Thornton and told him that a group of men were refusing duty. Soon after, the men themselves approached the captain, refusing to put to sea until they had a full complement. Thornton attempted to explain that he had no intention of sailing without a full complement, but he intended to cast off the quayside and anchor off shore so he could send his officers into the town to round up the missing crew. It was proving impossible to do this while alongside the quay, as no sooner were two or three crew located than another two or three took their chance to jump ship. Appeals to the group of men, both as a body and individually, proved fruitless.

After the gangway was drawn up, a crewman was observed to hoist his bag onto the quay and then lower himself after it. It was the pre-arranged signal for a mass exodus as, one by one, some thirty crewmen followed him. Each man was met with cheers from sympathisers ashore. The mutinous crew then took themselves off to the Sailor's Rest, where they staged an impromptu concert.

Thornton found himself in an impossible situation, unable to continue the voyage with his much depleted crew and running up expenses (including feeding the crew and passengers) of some £500 to £600 a day. After consulting with the White Star Line agents, he arranged for warrants to be issued for the charge of refusing duty. The superintendant at the Rest was instructed to put them up for the night, and at 1.30 a.m. twenty-seven of the fractious crew were rounded up by a sergeant and six constables. One more absconder was apprehended for intoxication and another two gave themselves up voluntarily. After appearing before the Fremantle Bench they were brought back to the *Belgic*, where only three continued to refuse duty. They were almost broke – the most any of them had in their pockets was a few shillings. James Freeman managed to success-fully argue that he was not a member of the *Belgic*'s crew as he was supposed to have been left behind in Cape Town, and was allowed to take his leave, which he did with some alacrity. The ringleaders were handed stiffer sentences and left ashore, while those who had returned to take up their duties were docked a day's pay.

Arriving in Adelaide, the emigrants experienced a mixture of relief and excitement, giving vent to their feelings about the issue with the food and the mutinous crew with the local papers. Thornton indignantly responded that most of the emigrants had never been treated so well in their lives, and gave some credence to the report of his 'scum of Europe' comment by further remarks to *The Advertiser*:

> It is a pity the Agents-General did not take more care in selecting the emigrants. They were a mixed lot, but the South Australian contingent I think were the best. There are always a number of 'copperheads' in any community, and when 2,000 people get together a gaol is always needed for some of them. No trouble whatever was experienced at sea, as there strict discipline can always be maintained, but when a crew get ashore and make straight for the public-house the trouble begins. Although there are some estimable people going to the eastern States the South Australian crowd is the best. Of course it was hard to keep the bad element from the good. Even at the table the roughs with their bad language were liable to contaminate the better class. It is regrettable that a country like Australia should not receive the best people for its citizens.

Putting aside the tribulations of their voyage, many of the new immigrants responded with curiosity and enthusiasm for their new

home. A Scotswoman, one of a party of twenty-six domestic servants looking for a new life in Australia, announced with exuberance
'Hurrah! I'm as happy as a sandboy.' Beaming, she admired the beautiful blue sky, but commented how hot it was. Told that it would be
even warmer in the summer, she responded 'I don't care, and I'm
jolly glad we're here.'[23]

But Thornton's trials were not over yet, and when on 26 November
the *Belgic* arrived in Sydney, the crew were still feeling rebellious. No
fewer than sixteen of them were now discharged by mutual con-
sent. Another eleven crew were unwilling to return home with the
Belgic and deserted in Sydney before she sailed. Replacements were
recruited and the *Belgic* returned home via Melbourne and Tilbury
docks, arriving in Liverpool on 21 February 1912. It was a voyage
Lowe would have been very glad to finish.

Not all was well at home. *Belgic* returned to find that the entire
shipping industry had been paralysed by a national coal strike that
had begun the previous month. Ships were idle and empty, moored
sometimes many abreast and it seemed Lowe's career was about to
be put on ice.

It was, but not in the way he expected. Within weeks he had
received a telegram notifying him peremptorily that he was being
assigned to a brand new ship. He was to report as soon as possible to
the White Star Line offices in Liverpool, there to pick up tickets for
an overnight crossing to Belfast. The ship he was instructed to join
was the RMS *Titanic*.

CHAPTER 6

A STRANGER TO
EVERYONE ON BOARD

Given the unique niche the *Titanic* occupies in the twenty-first century's popular imagination, it is difficult for us today to objectively assess the initial impression she made on her contemporaries and on the officers who served aboard her. Had it not been for the tragedy that befell her, she would most likely be remembered only as one of a series of impressive leviathans among many liners in the great age of steam.

Other liners, larger and more luxurious, were already under construction, a fact of which the *Titanic's* crew were well aware: 'Of course these two [*Olympic* and *Titanic*] are the largest in the world until our friends the Germans get their new *Imperator* afloat' wrote James Moody, one of the new officers. Even the notorious claim that she was 'practically unsinkable' was not new – such had been the original boast of the *Lusitania*, said by *The Shipbuilder* five years before to have 'Watertight bulkheads … arranged and fitted with the most stringent regard to making the vessel unsinkable.'

That the *Titanic* was a beautiful vessel there was no doubt. All the White Star Line ships manifested long graceful lines, belying their size, but she was nearly identical to the *Olympic*, launched the previous May. Nonetheless, for that slim window in time, she was indeed the largest and most luxurious ship afloat, even if she exceeded her sister ship's displacement by only 1,000 tons, at 46,500. '[T]he Titanic, Olympic and the Oceanic are going to be the 3 White Star ships on the S'ton – New York route for at least all next summer,' wrote Moody to his sister, 'unless of course any unforeseen diversion turns up.'[24]

When he first set eyes on her, hard-nosed Welshman Harold Lowe must have been singularly awed. Even with his 'experience of pretty well every ship afloat – from schooner to square-rigged sail, to steamships of all sizes', this vast vessel was beyond compare. She was fully four and a half times larger than the largest ship he'd ever been aboard. Moody also found himself at a loss when writing of the size of the RMS *Titanic*: 'I cannot describe any part of a ship which needs 85 clocks and 16 pianos to furnish it!'[25]

As the junior officers reported to their chief at noon on 24 March to sign on the ship's articles, one thing was already very apparent to Harold Lowe. The new fifth officer was very much the odd man out in a group of seven that constituted the *Titanic's* watchkeepers.

Chief Officer William Murdoch and officers Charles Lightoller, Herbert Pitman, Joseph Boxhall and James Moody had all served on the *Oceanic*, itself once the largest ship in the world at 17,000 tons. So had David Blair, soon to drop out of the crew for the main Atlantic crossing. Lowe's remarks on the subject reveal a deep consciousness that he was an outsider. He was very aware that most of his fellow officers had met many of their colleagues before and forged professional if not personal relationships. Lowe felt himself 'a total stranger in the ship and also to the run. I was a stranger to everyone on board.'[26]

Why Lowe was chosen to make the move from the small cargo and passenger vessels such as the *Tropic* and *Belgic* to the towering *Titanic* remains something of a mystery. His fellow officers, right down to the sixth, who had only been with the line for eight months, had all experienced both the Royal Mail Ships and the varied perils of the Western Ocean, as the Atlantic was poetically termed by the British. Perhaps his performance in helping to manage the quarrelsome Black Gang on the difficult *Belgic* voyage had been noted in his records.

A clue to White Star's selection methods was given at a Special Meeting held after the disaster:

Having fitted out this magnificent vessel, the '*Titanic*', we proceeded to man her with all that was best in the White Star organisation, and that, I believe, without boasting, means everything in the way of skill, manhood and *esprit de corps*. Whenever a man had distinguished himself in the service by means of ability and devotion to duty, he was earmarked at once to go to the '*Olympic*' or '*Titanic*', if it were possible to spare him from his existing position, with the result that, from Captain Smith, Chief Engineer Bell, Dr. O'Loughlin, Purser McElroy, Chief Steward Latimer, downwards, I can say without fear of contradiction, that a finer set of men never manned a ship, nor could be found in the whole of the Mercantile Marine of the country, and no higher testimony than this can be paid to the worth of any crew.[27]

The officers faced an immediate task after reporting to Murdoch – familiarising themselves with the mammoth dimensions of their new responsibility. For the remainder of the day, as James Moody explained to his sister, the juniors 'just played about the ship, learning the best way to get from one end to the other which I assure you takes quite a bit of finding.'[28]

Second Officer Lightoller told later how it took him a fortnight before he could confidently find his way to any location by the shortest route. He described how three of the junior officers spent an entire day attempting to find an aft starboard gangway door that was big enough to drive a horse and cart through. Which three officers, he doesn't say.

The builders and interior decorators worked around the officers as they walked the decks, hurrying to complete their tasks. Delays caused by the need to repair the *Olympic* following a collision with HMS *Hawke* meant that it was not anticipated they would be finished by the time the sea trials began. The clock for the forward Grand Staircase was not yet in place, the first-class dining-room tables needed their lamps, rooms were still being painted and the fine craftsmen that had been employed were adding the final touches to the sumptuously detailed interiors.

The rooms awaiting completion included the officers' quarters. These were located on the boat deck, immediately abaft the bridge, with Lowe's cabin on the port side. Above his quarters towered the first of the four vast funnels, each wide enough to accommodate two trains side by side. The officers noted with approval that although their cabins were small, they were not obliged to share and they had actual windows rather than portholes. Such touches made a difference.

During the decorating the officers were put up in one of Belfast's finest establishments, the Royal Avenue. This earned the exuberant approval of James Moody, who declared it a 'ripping hotel'.[29] Their work prior to sea trials was much the same as it had been in any other port – overseeing the provisioning and stowage and supervision of deck maintenance. There was little rest for anyone. Moody explained to his sister: 'We are awfully busy all day checking stores coming aboard.' Gear had to be checked and certified, and all made ready for her maiden sailing.

On 1 April a celebrated skipper came aboard. His reputation preceded him: 'The famous E.J. Smith,' as the youngest officer referred to him in a letter, adding that 'though I believe he's an awful stickler for discipline, he's popular with everybody.'[30] Smith had reportedly once described his career with the White Star Line as 'uneventful', but the coming together of the *Olympic* and the *Hawke* might have caused him to review his remark. The *Olympic* was under pilotage at the time and the collision was not held to be the responsibility of Smith himself but it underlined the difficulties of handling the new breed of mammoth liners.

With his genial personality and reputation for discipline, not to mention his marvellous Edward VII beard, Smith personified the captain that was respected by passengers and crew alike. He knew how to keep the line happy, and he welded his commands to the rigid schedule of the mail run. Lightoller, who served under Smith on the *Majestic*, noted that he had a soft voice that he rarely raised, but when required he could 'bark an order that made a man come to himself with a bump.'

There would be another new arrival at Southampton with Henry Wilde coming aboard as chief officer and Murdoch dropping down to first. David Blair left the ship altogether. ('Luckily for him as it turned out,' Lightoller wryly observed.) Henry Tingle Wilde was the tallest of the *Titanic*'s officers, standing 6ft 1in, and was by all accounts a physically powerful man. Yet privately he cut a rather tragic figure. Born in Liverpool, he would never know his father, who died of hepatitis (aged only thirty-four) some three and a half months before he was born. Wilde married Mary 'Polly' Jones, but in December 1910 came the bitter blow of the death of twin infant sons after a very difficult birth. Polly lingered in what must have been excruciating agony but died that Christmas Eve. When his appointment to the *Titanic* came through, Wilde was initially reluctant to accept. 'I still don't like this ship,' he wrote to his sister, 'I have a queer feeling about it.'[31]

Now acting as first officer, William Murdoch was a thirty-nine-year-old Scot who seems to have been something of a seafaring prodigy. Alone among the *Titanic*'s officers, Murdoch had never failed a Board of Trade examination and had taken his Second and First Mates' certificates within days of signing off ships and without recourse to cram schools.

Murdoch had served as Smith's first officer since 1908, the two making successful maiden voyages on the *Adriatic* in 1907 and the *Olympic* in 1911. Coupled with his experience and talent was an affable personality that won him respect and popularity within the small elite group of White Star officers. One of his friends, Edwin Jones, was many years later to relate to others, including students he taught in Melbourne and to historian and author Geoffrey Marcus, an anecdote that served to illustrate both the perils of service on the mail boats and Murdoch's superlative skills and judgement. One night while the two men were serving on the *Arabic*, Murdoch came on deck to take his watch. He found a slight mist in the air and deceptive conditions of visibility. Before he had quite gained his night vision and taken over the watch from the first officer, a light was reported on the port bow. The officer of the watch, Fox, ordered 'Watch your port helm' (an order prefacing an alteration of course to starboard) without seeing the light himself. Murdoch at the same moment saw a red light almost under the *Arabic*'s bows and realised that there was no time to alter course. Without time to explain his actions, he rushed to the wheel and pushed the quartermaster, who had already begun to port the helm, to one side. He returned the wheel and held her to the course.

The men instinctively ducked as a large sailing vessel, with all sails set and the wind on her port quarters, swept past them so close that it seemed her yardarms would sweep the bridge. After a few moments' silence, Murdoch told Jones, 'Go and steady her on.' His swift appraisal of the situation and action had averted a collision.[32] Jones was to remember Murdoch's handling of the incident – and Murdoch himself – with a sense of respect and not a little awe. 'There was never a better officer. Cool, capable, on his toes always – and smart toes they were.'[33] Of the trio of most senior officers – Smith, Wilde and Murdoch – one man who knew them was to write, 'Mr Wilde, the Chief Officer, and Mr Murdock [*sic*], the first mate, were splendid types of men, and old Captain Smith was beloved by everyone.'[34]

Charles Herbert Lightoller, second officer, would eventually win fame as the most recognised *Titanic* officer after the captain. As the senior surviving officer, his autobiography and subsequent treatment in books and cinema earned him a large popular following, but Lowe himself, as we will see, might have had ambivalent feelings towards his senior.

Herbert John Pitman, third officer, came from a background far removed from the sea. A native of Somerset, his family had been farmers for centuries. But he had an amiable nature and a way of dealing with passengers that made him an asset to the line he had

served since joining the *Gothic* as her third officer in May 1907. He
had survived a shipwreck, an incident he described as a 'minor affair.'

Joseph Boxhall, at twenty-eight the closest in age to Lowe, was the
son of a Hull sea captain of the Wilson Line, also named Joseph. He
stood slightly taller than Lowe and was slim and dark. Boxhall, fourth
officer, was already establishing a reputation as a very promising navi-
gator and was described in a Hull newspaper as a 'wonderfully smart
young officer.' Once, as a young apprentice in sail, Boxhall had been
hauling ropes during heavy weather when a violent sea crashed him
to the deck and badly injured his leg. The lad struggled to his feet and
finished his watch before seeking treatment.

If Murdoch and Boxhall represented the traditional merchant
officer, one virtually born into the career, Sixth Officer James Paul
Moody represented another model: that of no seafaring background
at all. The only officer junior to Lowe, twenty-four-year-old Moody
was a bright lad from a distinguished Scarborough family that had
gone through a difficult period and the dispersal of his immediate
family. After the death of his mother in 1898 when he was only
eleven years old, the relatives charged with his care sought a means
of finishing his education and providing him with a livelihood. At
fourteen he was sent to HMS *Conway*, a training ship that educated
many sons of the professional classes for careers at sea.

'Lots of people,' he observed on an early voyage, 'have put in their
letters how they would love to be seeing all the beautiful places I am
seeing, but I tell them to stop at home or else invent a floating palace
which doesn't roll and can't possibly sink.'[35]

The *Titanic* completed her sea trials at Belfast. Lowe was so
impressed with the vessel that he believed she could 'easily do 24
or 25 knots,' adding that 'on the trials the *Titanic* behaved splendidly
and manoeuvred very well.' Later events would call into question
that manoeuvrability, but the ship was never designed to execute
tight evasive actions. Her domain was the open sea, save for times
when harbour tugs nudged her in and out of port.

Trials over, there was time to write a few postcards to friends and
family. Lowe also took one of the *Titanic* menus of 2 April, scrawling
across the bottom 'The first meal ever served on board' before post-
ing it to Nellie.

The imperious new vessel set sail that evening at 8 p.m., bound
for Southampton. It berthed in the early hours of 4 April, Moody

recording in a letter written later that day, 'Arrived here safely at
1.30am after a fine weather passage from Belfast. Docked by moon-
light…'[36] The *Titanic* would have eleven more days to live.

At 8 a.m. on the morning of her arrival the crew 'hoisted a huge
rainbow of flags right over the ship, 220 flags 9 feet apart.'[37] It was
a salute to the people of Southampton, as in order to complete the
necessary work to the interiors the vessel could not be opened to
sightseers as the *Olympic* had entertained them the previous year,
with a small charge for charity.

On 5 April Lowe sent Nellie a postcard of the ship from
Southampton. The card consisted of typical pre-sailing banalities
and closed with, 'Will write tonight. Kind regards to all.'[38]

Sailing day, 10 April. The crew mustered at 8.30 a.m.. Lowe and
Moody attended the Board of Trade inspection of the lifeboats, a
process requiring two of the starboard boats to be lowered, each
with a complement of crew. After a turn around the dock, the boats
returned and were hoisted back on deck.

Each department was meanwhile being kept busy in preparation
for departure. Engine and deck crew toiled at propulsion and navigation checks, while victualling staff were already hard at work for
the embarking passengers.

First class, second and steerage all came on board – by separate
gangways, naturally – each social rank familiarising themselves with
their accommodations and the services available. The usual mix of
tact and discretion from the stewards, White Star's equivalent of a
hotel staff, saw everyone made as comfortable as possible.

The new ship cast off at midday to little fanfare. There were scant
dockside scenes, apart from the odd tearful farewell and a last-
minute dash by some stokers who had lingered too long over their
going-away pints, alcohol being forbidden to the crew at sea.

Lowe was on the bridge, working the telephones that connected
Pilot George Bowyer and Captain Smith with Lightoller on the
stem and Murdoch aft. The ships stranded in port, still penned by the
coal strike, meant an even defter touch than usual was required to
ease the ship's progress into the Solent.

The *New York*, tied to the *Oceanic*, succumbed to the insidious
pull of the monster sliding past, first straining and then snapping the
lines that moored her. Drawn towards the black hull, it seemed collision was inevitable, but swift work by the men on the *Titanic* and

nearby tugs averted the danger as the smaller vessel was brought to heel. There was a pause, and then the *Titanic* crept ahead once more, bound for the English Channel.

Cherbourg was first port of call, a matter of a few hours' steaming. Tenders ferried passengers out to the ship, among them the most illustrious names of the passenger list. A day later, 11 April, the *Titanic* called at Queenstown in Ireland, where she embarked over 100 emigrant steerage.

As the Irish coast slipped from view, the ship began to settle into a routine. For some wealthier passengers it meant the end of the Grand Tour, for others it was an irrevocable abandonment of their old lives for the promise of betterment. But for the crew, new vessel or no, it was a simply another voyage.

Murdoch now made out the emergency boat lists, assigning men to their theoretical positions in case of emergency. Lowe handled the document on its way to the captain, glancing at it 'casually'. From this brief perusal he noticed that there were only three seamen assigned to some boats and four to others. It is a racing certainty that Lowe paid more attention to the sheets than their ultimate recipient.

The days turned over, each man shaking down into his duties, the weather blessedly clear. On the evening of Sunday 14 April, Lowe entered onto the bridge for the second dog watch, lasting from 6–8 p.m. The night, he observed, was 'fine and clear, bright overhead and dark on the water; calm wind and sea.'[39]

The telegraph indicated Full Ahead. Lightoller, the officer of the watch, was assessing ice warnings of the type the ship had been receiving for several days now. Lightoller worked out that they would be up to the ice at 9.30 p.m. The information does not appear to have overly worried Harold Lowe.

He had more immediate matters of concern. The junior officer relieving had to ring up the engine room to get the revolutions for the last watch. As he worked on a dead reckoning position (an estimation of position based on course, time and speed) to be handed to the captain at 8 p.m., Lowe glanced up and noticed a chit of paper pinned to the chart.

'Ice,' it declared, noting a few co-ordinates. Lowe did some mental arithmetic and confirmed to his own satisfaction that Lightoller was right and they would not be in its vicinity until after his watch was over.

The temperature had been falling, but Lowe did not particularly notice it; he was busy with a slate of humdrum tasks. He had seen bergs before, on those long voyages around the Horn.

As Lowe worked in the chartroom, Lightoller took star fixes, Officer Pitman at his side jotting them down. The unusual clarity allowed for excellent sights. Pitman now took the set of co-ordinates to work out their position from the celestial observations. His findings would be compared with Lowe's dead reckoning for a composite position to set before the master.

The sea stretched out like glass and it was almost preternaturally calm. An air of serenity prevailed in the chart room and wheelhouse. Lowe observed that 'the weather ... was splendid. It was a fine clear night with no wind. There was no moon but the stars were shining brilliant and they could be seen rising and setting on the horizon. There was no fog or haze and the sea appeared quite calm. It was cold.'[40]

Eight o'clock duly came, and Lowe could stand down.

Boxhall and Moody were coming on duty now, the staggering of the junior and senior watches meaning that Lightoller, the senior man, still had another two hours before he could turn in to a warm bunk on this increasingly cold night.

Pitman cheerfully handed over Lightoller's sightings to Boxhall: 'Here's a bunch of sights for you, Old Man. Go ahead.' Lowe and Moody's words are lost, but hardly amounted to anything eventful. Lowe then left and turned towards his cabin.

He climbed straight into his bunk and was very soon asleep. He would next have to wake at midnight for the long trick until 4 a.m. Elsewhere in the vessel the Widener dinner party was winding down in the first-class dining room, and the passengers too began to turn in. A few hardy souls braved the coldness of the night as the ship ploughed westward on smooth seas.

Lowe slumbered deeply. 'We don't get any too much sleep, and when we sleep we die,' he later insisted.

And in that sleep of death, what dreams may come? When Lowe was to wake four hours later, it was to enter into a living nightmare.

CHAPTER 7

MAYHEM ON
THE TITANIC

Voices roused him from slumber. They were loud, urgent, unusual. For a few moments he lay half awake, listening. They were the voices of passengers, and they were out of place. Lowe leapt out of bed and soon knew something was badly wrong. His feet, for one thing, told him that the ship was tipping down by the head. Lowe walked out into the middle of a seaman's worst nightmare. Passengers in lifebelts were scurrying about, the crew clearing away lifeboats.

At around 11.40 p.m., as Lowe slept, the crisis had begun with a chilling caress. A shape loomed out of the night, a 'black thing' that would haunt lookout Fred Fleet for many years thereafter. The telephone rang sharply in the wheelhouse, answered by Sixth Officer James Moody.

Moody, already alerted to something in their path by the signal of three bells from the Crow's Nest, asked the lookout: 'What do you see?'

'Iceberg, right ahead.'

'Thank you.'

First Officer Murdoch ordered hard-a-starboard. He was intending a further hard-a-port to stage an emergency slalom around the berg. But the helm responded too slowly, and the vessel under his command groaned into contact with ice on her starboard side.

The scrape led to seams in five compartments being opened to the sea. Murdoch now closed the watertight doors, but the bulkheads below him only went as high as E-deck – and were open at the top – so the fate of the ship was already out of his hands.

Captain Smith arrived on the bridge, demanding: 'What have we hit?' The carpenter was already on his way to the bridge to inform the officers that the forward compartments were making water: one, two, three.

Fourth Officer Boxhall dashed from the bridge to see the damage. He quickly met one of the postal workers, who told him that the mail hold was flooding. He saw men struggling to move sacks out of the sorting room as bags of letters floated around their knees. All this Boxhall flew back to tell the bridge. He was sent to rouse his fellow officers.

Lightoller and Pitman he found already awake and waiting in their cabins, aware something was amiss since the ship had stopped. Boxhall called in at Lowe, but the latter, in his dead of sleep, slept on.

Awareness spread. The engineers and firemen learned pretty smartly. Leading Stoker Thomas Threlfall took ten firemen and four trimmers to tend to the boilers in his section. All of them felt distinctly uneasy, but carried out their duty as ordered, drawing the fires. 'It did not feel nice going down below, because we knew a bad accident had happened,' he said.

Able Seaman Joseph Scarrott had heard the three peals. When the collision came the shock was 'not so great as one would expect,' but he rushed down to alert his mate in any case. The friend was using the head near the foot of the ladder. 'Give me a call if anything's doing,' said the otherwise-occupied crewman.

Scarrott ran up on deck with those men who had turned out from their bunks. They found large amounts of ice scattered on the forward well deck. At length they could see no real cause for alarm, and receiving no orders, went back below, some to their bunks. They had not been there long when the Bosun barged in. 'Big Nick' Nicholls boomed: 'All hands on deck! Turn out the boats! Covers off and stow amidships.' They tumbled out again.

Scarrott still believed it was a precaution. The sooner it was done, the quicker he could get to his bunk. He began clearing the boats, before Chief Officer Wilde ordered him to go to his own station – Lifeboat 14.

In second class, Nellie Walcroft and Clear Annie Cameron had been in bed since 10.30 p.m. They were emigrating to America to work as domestic servants to the richest families they could find. Nellie was jolted awake, and roused her friend: 'Clear, what's that?'

'Oh, nothing. I suppose it's the lads, off to bed.'

Nellie knew it wasn't. 'I was nearly thrown out of my berth,' she exclaimed. They noticed the engines had stopped. Outside they could hear running and voices. Looking into the corridor, they encountered a steward who called out: 'Go back to your beds, no danger!' They did so, unconvinced.

A little later they heard a man's voice outside their cabin say 'an iceberg' as it passed. 'Nell, out of it, we'd better see what's the matter,' said Clear. 'Put your clothes on sharp, don't talk.'[41]

In her first-class cabin on C Deck, New Yorker Irene 'Rene' Harris and her theatre producer husband Henry were still up. Rene could not sleep because of the pain in her arm, which she had fractured earlier that day in a fall. When the ship stopped she noticed the garments hanging up in the cabin cease their rhythmic sway with the ship's motion.

Lowe finally emerged into a nicely matured maelstrom. He saw the captain fleetingly. Someone he stopped told him the ship had struck an iceberg. Lowe moved to the starboard side, to where Boat 7 was already being loaded under the command of First Officer Murdoch.

The boat was loaded with women and children – and some men. Murdoch was to show consistently more latitude to men on the starboard side than the short shrift Second Officer Lightoller was dispensing on the port. It was difficult enough to get the boats filled in these very early stages, with the big ship clearly a better bet than a helpless cockleshell in many minds. Boat 7 was eventually lowered – the first away of the night – and Murdoch and Lowe went forward to Boat 5, where Third Officer Pitman would eventually take charge.

Passenger Charles Stengel had just loaded his wife into Boat 5, when he saw two men, Dr Henry Frauenthal and his brother Isaac, jump into the boat. Dr Frauenthal, a corpulent man, landed atop Annie May Stengel. Mrs Stengel cried out that he had broken her ribs.

Not only the Stengels were furious, but Lowe too. He announced, 'I will stop that. I will go down and get my gun.'[42]

Lowe was gone only 'momentarily' and returned brandishing a Browning automatic, his personal firearm. He had been interested in firearms from an early age, and now it would prove a useful prop. The senior officers would later be issued with Webley revolvers from the ship's armoury as the situation worsened.

Lowe, when later asked why he went for his gun, replied: 'You never know when you will need it,' but the sight of the weapon, rather than any threat of use, would do at this stage to deter anyone from defying orders.

There was still manifest faith in the ship's buoyancy. Her slow settling was doing little to shake passengers out of their trust in publicity puffs about bulkheads and watertight doors. The first-class men, in any case, were wedded to ostentatious displays of sang-froid. 'Oh she's good for eight hours yet,' said one. He was among the more pessimistic.

1. Harold Godfrey Lowe in RNR Rating's Uniform, c.1904. (Lowe Family Collection, John Lowe)

2. Crew of the *Ormsary* at Newcastle, Australia, in August 1903. Lowe is seated front row, fourth from left. (Lowe Family Collection, John Lowe)

3. Ellen 'Nellie' Whitehouse, *c*.1912. (Lowe Family Collection, John Lowe)

4. Deck officers of the SS *Addah*, *c*.1909. Captain Hough seated centre front row, Second Officer Harold Lowe standing back row, far right. (The Lowe Family Collection, John Lowe)

R.M.S. "TITANIC."

APRIL 2, 1912.

HORS D'ŒUVRE VARIÉS

CONSOMMÉ MIRRETTE
CREAM OF CHICKEN

SALMON

SWEETBREADS

ROAST CHICKEN
SPRING LAMB, MINT SAUCE
BRAISED HAM & SPINACH

GREEN PEAS   CAULIFLOWER
BOVIN & BOILED POTATOES

GOLDEN PLOVER ON TOAST
SALAD

PUDDING SANS SOUCI
PEACHES IMPERIAL
PASTRY

DESSERT   COFFEE

The first meal ever served on board

5. *Above:* This postcard, purchased in Belfast, was kept by Lowe as a souvenir. Although the vessel is actually modelled on the *Titanic's* sister *Olympic*, the caption suggests it is the *Titanic*. Sixth Officer James Moody sent a similar one to his family, noting that: 'This is, of course, rather a faked photo as this ship has never been through the water & the background shows New York, but it's a very good likeness.' (Lowe Family Collection, John Lowe)

6. *Left:* The menu that Lowe sent to Nellie with the words, 'The first meal ever served on board', written across it. (John Creamer Collection, Inger Sheil)

7. Sixth Officer James Paul Moody of the *Titanic*. He worked side by side with Lowe loading and launching lifeboats. (Private collection, Inger Sheil)

8. Second-class passenger Selena Rogers Cook, who left the *Titanic* in Lifeboat 14. She was later to say of Lowe that 'too much praise cannot be given the officer', and that she and the others in the boat owed their lives to him. (Philip Gowan Collection, Inger Sheil)

9. John Herbert Pitman as depicted in the *Washington Times*, 23 April 1912. (Photograph courtesy of Senan Molony)

10. Joseph Groves Boxhall. (Photograph courtesy of Senan Molony, © The Bell Album)

REAL HERO OF THE TITANIC

How Survivors, Drifting in Open Boats, Were Saved

"If Great Britain had only such seamen as Fifth Officer Lowe, there would be no such disasters. He is the hero of the survivors of the Titanic. He is a brave, splendid man, whom Great Britain should reward by instant promotion. When I praised him for his courage, he said: 'I have only done my duty. I only hollered. Anybody can holler.'"—MRS. RENEE HARRIS.

By ADA PATTERSON.

MRS. RENEE HARRIS.

One of the widows of the Titanic told me her story yesterday.

Black garbed, her right arm immovable in its plaster cast, her dark eyes staring with the same melancholy horror on the scenes she summoned as she had looked upon the realities that black night of April 14, Mrs. Renee Harris lay on a couch in her drawing room. Upon the back of the couch rested a photograph of her husband, Henry B. Harris, who sank with the doomed ship. On the piano opposite stood another photograph. Resting against it was a card that had accompanied one of his last gifts to her, a gift she cherished less than the inscription on it: "To my only sweetheart on the twelfth anniversary of our wedding."

"I feel as though I had died and that my dear husband's spirit was in me and I was here to try to do what he would have done," she said in a plaintive contralto voice, in this her first interview. She looked at the easy, relaxed sitting figure and the pleasant

...ce pictured in the frame on the piano. "My boy," she said as though ...hat picture were a presence. "My ...

Mrs. Harris, who was widowed when the Titanic sank, tells how the brave young little officer, a

11. Irene 'Renee' Harris, first-class *Titanic* passenger, rescued in Collapsible D. Harris, who lost her husband in the disaster, was one of Lowe's staunchest admirers. She proclaimed him: 'The real hero of the Titanic' – a view she reiterated twenty years later. This newspaper clipping was among Harold Lowe's papers. (Courtesy Lowe Family Collection, Inger Sheil)

12. *Left:* Third-class passenger Rhoda Abbott, pictured in 1928. She was the only woman to go into the water and survive after climbing into Collapsible A but her two young sons died in the sinking. She was to say that 'had it not been for Officer Lowe, I would have been drowned. I was nearly exhausted when he lifted me into his lifeboat.' (Philip Gowan Collection, Inger Sheil)

13. *Below: New York Evening Journal* illustration of Lowe at the tiller of Lifeboat 14. (Courtesy Lowe Family Collection, Inger Sheil)

The lifeboat commanded by Mr. Lowe, the fifth officer of the Titanic, who rigged a sail and transferred passengers so that at daybreak he took on board from an overturned collapsible boat 20 men and one woman.

14. A further image of Lowe at the tiller of Lifeboat 14, after having lowered the sail. (Courtesy Lowe Family Collection, Inger Sheil)

15 and 16. Two men from Michigan who were to have a significant impact on the American investigation into the tragedy, and on the life of Harold Lowe: Senator William Alden Smith and his friend and supporter Sheriff Joseph Bayliss. Lowe's relationship with Smith was adversarial in nature, but in Bayliss he found a kindred spirit. (Library of Congress Prints and Photographs Division Washington, DC / Joseph Bayliss Public Library. Inger Sheil)

17. Lowe arrives in Liverpool on the *Adriatic* to be met by his father George and sister, Ada. (Lowe Family Collection, John Lowe)

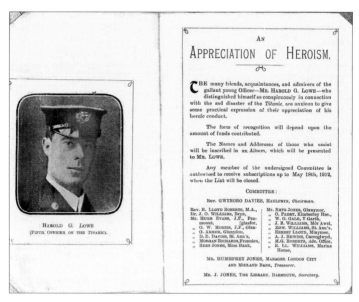

AN
APPRECIATION OF HEROISM.

THE many friends, acquaintances, and admirers of the gallant young Officer—Mr. HAROLD G. LOWE—who distinguished himself so conspicuously in connection with the sad disaster of the *Titanic*, are anxious to give some practical expression of their appreciation of his heroic conduct.

The form of recognition will depend upon the amount of funds contributed.

The Names and Addresses of those who assist will be inscribed in an Album, which will be presented to MR. LOWE.

Any member of the undersigned Committee is authorised to receive subscriptions up to May 18th, 1912, when the List will be closed.

COMMITTEE :

Rev. GWYNORO DAVIES, HAULFRYN, *Chairman.*

Rev. R. LLOYD ROBERTS, M.A.,	Mr. RHYS JONES, Glanymor,
Dr. J. O. WILLIAMS, Bryn,	„ O. PARRY, Kimberley Hse.,
Mr. HUGH EVANS, J.P., Penmount,	„ W. G. GALE, Y Garth,
[glasfor,	„ J. R. WILLIAMS, Môr Awel,
„ O. W. MORRIS, J.P., Glan-	„ EDW. WILLIAMS, St. Ann's,
„ O. ARMER, Glanydon,	„ ERNEST LLOYD, Minymor,
„ D. E. DAVIES, St. Ann's,	„ A. J. HEWINS, Carreglwyd,
„ MORGAN RICHARDS,Fronolen,	„ M.G. ROBERTS, *Ade.* Office,
„ REES JONES, Moss Bank,	„ R. LL. WILLIAMS, Marine House,

MR. HUMHPREY JONES, MANAGER LONDON CITY AND MIDLAND BANK, *Treasurer.*

MR. J. JONES, THE LIBRARY, BARMOUTH, *Secretary.*

HAROLD G. LOWE
(FIFTH OFFICER ON THE *TITANIC*).

18. Pamphlet distributed through Barmouth in April–May 1912. The generous public response enabled the gift of an engraved gold watch, presented to Lowe in a ceremony hosted by the town. The accompanying photograph shows Lowe in his Elder Dempster uniform. (Tom Hughes Collection, Inger Sheil)

19. *Left:* Lowe with his two children, Harold and Josie, taken in 1917 shortly before he joined the crew of HMS *Suffolk*. (Lowe Family Collection, John Lowe)

20. *Below:* RMS *Titanic*, pencil sketch by Harold Lowe. The image is undated but the handling of the funnels suggest it is one of his later works. Based on a photograph of the ship at anchor, he has added a bow way and smoke from all funnels (including, erroneously, the 'dummy' fourth funnel) to suggest that she is underway, as well as the American flag at her foremast to indicate destination. (Lowe Family Collection, John Lowe)

21. On board the deck of HMS *Suffolk* deep in the Siberian winter, with the ship's dog Puppsie cradled in his arms. (Lowe Family Collection, John Lowe)

22. Crew of the HMS *Suffolk*. (Lowe Family Collection, John Lowe)

23. Lt Harold Lowe with a shore party in Vladivostok. He captioned this picture, 'Toughs', and a similar one was labelled 'More toughs'. (Lowe Family Collection)

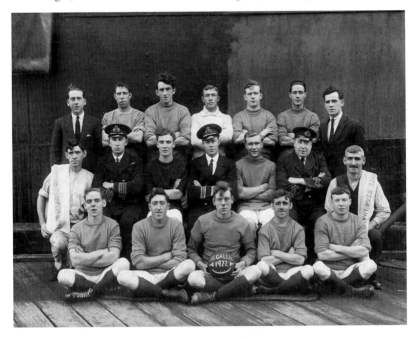

24. Chief Officers of RMS *Gallic*. (Lowe Family Collection, John Lowe)

THE
INVINCIBLE
2ND

25. Caricature of 'The Invincible Second'. (Lowe Family Collection, John Lowe)

26. Lowe looking out to sea in his summer whites. (Lowe Family Collection, John Lowe)

27. *Above:* Lowe in the 1920s as a Valentino-inspired Sheik and a passenger in costume for one of the quintessential shipboard events: the costume party. (Lowe Family Collection, John Lowe)

28. Chief Officer Lowe, sextant in hand, ubiquitous pipe in place. (Lowe family Collection, John Lowe)

29. First Officer Lowe supervising a lifeboat drill on RMS *Doric*, 5 November 1929. (Lowe Family Collection, John Lowe)

30. Harold and Nellie on the Conway River in *Pirate* following Harold's retirement. (Lowe Family Collection, John Lowe)

31. Lowe in 'civilian' clothes. Portrait taken by a fellow Mason. (Lowe Family Collection, John Lowe)

32. Harold Lowe seated second from right on the dais with fellow councillors as Prime Minister Lloyd George opens a local community centre. (Lowe Family Collection, John Lowe)

33. Harold Lowe, confined to a bath chair following his stroke, in the garden of his Deganwy home, 1944. (Lowe Family Collection, John Lowe)

'They speak of the bravery of the men. I do not think there was any particular bravery, because none of the men thought it was going down. If they had, they would not have frivoled as they did about it,' Mrs White told the American inquiry.[43] Meanwhile the officers themselves were downplaying the seriousness of the situation. Stengel said they 'showed very good judgment.' He explained, 'I think they were very cool. They calmed the passengers by making them believe it was not a serious accident.' One of the four surviving officers, unidentified, later told him, 'Suppose we had reported the damage that was done to that vessel; there would not be one of you aboard [the rescue ship *Carpathia*.] The [stokers] would have come up and taken every boat.'[44]

Trying to forestall a panic, the officers did little to instil a sense of urgency into the passengers, their potential recruits for precious places. Lowe shouted for more women and children at Boat 5, but when none came forward Officer Murdoch ordered the boat lowered.

Third Officer Herbert Pitman was ordered to take it away from the ship. As it creaked towards the inky well, Pitman blew his whistle to get the men on deck to stop lowering. He wanted to see if the plug – normally left out to allow rainwater drain from a lifeboat – had been put back. An irritated officer yelled from above, 'It is your own blooming business to see that the plug is in!'[45]

J. Bruce Ismay, managing director of the White Star Line, was getting impatient too. Privately appraised of the seriousness of the situation, he had been given to understand that the ship had only an hour to live. As a result he was frantically shooing passengers towards the boats.

Lowe, kneeling on the deck in the hard work of handling the falls and perhaps already irritated by Pitman, looked up to see a male passenger holding onto a davit with one arm and wheeling the other in a circle, urging him in a loud voice, 'Lower away, lower away!'

Not having any idea of the identity or importance of this gentleman, Lowe suddenly reared up in indignation. 'If you'll get the hell out of it, I'll be able to do something,' he snarled. 'You want me to lower away quickly? You'll have me drown the whole lot of them!'[46]

Ismay, chastened, turned away to the next boat without saying a word. Lowe continued his work unimpeded and Boat 5 reached the water and rowed away. It was sparsely occupied.

Murdoch and Lowe moved forward to Boat 3. It was at this moment that Lowe first became aware of distress rockets screaming upwards into the night. One exploded overhead, nearly deafening him, bathing the decks in fitful illumination.

Although the heroic efforts of the engineers kept the *Titanic*'s lights burning until minutes before her end, Lowe had difficulties in the dim light of the boat deck, far from the richly lit saloons of the interior. The ship's assistant surgeon, Jack Simpson, brought him an electric torch, muttering, 'Here is something that will be useful to you.' He melted back into the crowd as Lowe gratefully accepted the gift.[47]

The conduct of the passengers remained generally good and without a sense of urgency. But there were irksome problems, Lowe remembered. 'The people were messing up the falls, getting foul of the falls, and I had to halloa a bit to get them off.' The 'halloaing' may not have been as genteel as the phrase suggests.[48]

Lifeboat 1, the most forward starboard boat, would become the most notoriously under-filled of the evening. An emergency cutter with a capacity of forty, she was launched with complement of twelve. Of these, only five were passengers, and two women.

Lady Duff Gordon recalled that when her husband asked 'Might we get into this boat?' the officer in charge responded 'in a very polite way indeed.' His reported words sound rather too polite for the previously vexed Harold Lowe: 'Oh certainly; do; I will be very pleased.' Some inaccurate reports had him gallantly asking: 'Lady Gordon [sic] are you ready?'

It should be pointed out that the Duff Gordons were travelling incognito under the alias Morgan. Lowe, never terribly *au fait* with the Edwardian glitterati, maintained, 'I simply bundled her into the boat.' After calling several times for more passengers, Lowe and Murdoch lowered what would become known as the 'Millionaires' Lifeboat'.

Passenger Stengel was one of the handful aboard, pursuing his wife's boat into the night. An officer had told him to jump in, he said. He tumbled into the boat in such an ungainly fashion that the officer laughed heartily and remarked either, 'That is the funniest sight I have seen to-night' or 'that is the funniest manoeuvre yet.'

Rather than shame or embarrassment, Stengel felt a surge of optimism. He was 'greatly encouraged' by the words, which suggested that the situation was not so serious. The officer either 'did not think there was much danger or he disguised his belief of danger completely.' It would have been typical of Lowe to make an irreverent remark on the spur of the moment. A comparatively late arrival on the boat deck himself, his own state of knowledge was certainly less complete than that of Ismay.

With the comparatively swift loading and lowering of boats 7, 5, 3 and 1, half the boats on the starboard side – the four furthest forward – had been launched. The *Titanic* famously carried only sixteen life-boats in all, with another four collapsibles stowed forward.

Why did the officers not fill the boats to their capacity – 65.5, as Lowe would later precisely note? The boats would have held in excess of seventy people, as tests at builders Harland & Wolff had demonstrated. Moreover, the boats themselves carried plates near their bows explicitly stating the numbers that could be taken. The testimony of the surviving officers was consistent as to their igno-rance of the safe limits. They feared the davits would not take the weight, unaware that the new Welin davits were designed to do so.

At the height of the crisis, Officer Lightoller improvised a plan to fill the boats to a full floating capacity once they had reached the water. He ordered Bosun Nicholls and ten men to go below and open the gangway doors in the ship's sides. The idea proved a disaster. Once reaching the surface of the ocean the boats almost all pulled away immediately, and none succeeded in loading passengers from the gangway.

The sight must have dismayed the senior officers and the captain. Boat 6, under the direction of Quartermaster Robert Hichens, even went so far as to ignore orders hailed through a megaphone to return. Hichens announced to his flock: 'It's our lives now, not theirs.'

Lowe said he 'overheard a conversation referring to the gangway doors being opened, and that the bosun and a crowd of men had been sent down there.' He thus continued to load and lower the boats at under-capacity, ordering each to 'haul off from the ship's side, but remain within hail.'[49]

As he worked at Boat 1, word was passed around that a ship had been sighted on the port bow. Glancing in that direction, Lowe saw what he believed was a steamer showing the red light of her port side. She was about 5 miles off, he concluded. As Lowe observed the lights off the bow, his colleagues were to summon the stranger, sending by Morse lamp: '*We are the* Titanic *sinking*.' The ship did not respond.

CHAPTER 8

LAUNCHING
LIFEBOAT 14

After loading Boat 1, Lowe made his way diagonally all the way aft on the port side. Here the loading of Boats 12, 14 and 16 was already well underway. There was already a crowd gathered, and a greater sense of urgency. Many foreign-tongued steerage had begun swelling the area, causing difficulties and frustration, not least in communication.

Clear Cameron, standing there, thought 'there was no excitement or fuss of any kind.'[50] There was, however, something of a general push towards the boats and some individuals were beginning to feel the cold touch of desperation. An element of unruliness entered the picture, and Seaman Scarrott had to shout and wield a boat's tiller to hold off the crowd.

He had to use 'a bit of persuasion,' said Scarrott, and Seaman John Poingdestre backed him up in testifying that the passengers at 12 and 14 were trying to rush the boats. He too tried to keep them back 'to the best of my ability.'

Faced with the crushing around the boats, Lowe held his Browning high and barked commands to bring the throng to order. He insisted he was prepared to use the gun. There would be a strict policy of women and children first, he told them, and men were to step back from the boats. The weapon drew all eyes.

They shrank back, apart from one first-class passenger – 'a rich nabob' – who, according to Lowe, tried several times to disobey orders and join his wife in a lifeboat. Lowe levelled his gun and told him with an accompanying expletive that he could 'chase himself around the deck' if he thought he was getting in. First class could expect no preferential treatment and Lowe later prided himself that the wealthy had to take their chances with the other passengers and female crew at his station. 'There was no such thing as selecting. It was simply the first woman, whether first class, second class, or sixty-seventh class. It was all the same; women and children were first.'[51]

Alexander Compton, another first-class male, escorted his mother Mary and sister Sara to the boat deck and assisted them into 14. He then turned to Lowe and asked if he might be permitted to accompany the women. Lowe was adamant: no men. Compton stepped back without complaint.

Daisy Minahan, travelling first class with her doctor brother William and his wife Lillian, stumbled over loaves of bread that had been brought on deck by the bakers for the lifeboats. She and Lillian entered Boat 14, but William had to stand back and prepare to die. Daisy would later question Fifth Officer Lowe's personal conduct, even his sobriety, whereas Sara Compton developed profound admiration for the man who had prevented her brother from entering a boat.

Clear Cameron and Nellie Walcroft made their way to the area, with Clear indignant to find no senior officer in charge. 'There was no Captain and no First Officer to be seen, just two young Officers [Lowe and Sixth Officer James Moody] shouting and giving orders for women and children to get into the boats as quickly as they can, all the men stand back – which they did without a murmur, poor souls, helping their wives and children and saying "Goodbye".[52] Nellie and Clear entered Boat 14 as Daisy Minahan recalled 'the voluble officers 'yelling and cursing at men to stand back and let the women get into the boats.'

Charlotte Collyer, a second-class emigrant, was struck by Lowe's appearance and energy: 'Mr Lowe was very young and boyish-looking; but somehow he compelled people to obey him. He rushed among the passengers and ordered the women into the boat. Many of them followed him in a dazed kind of way, but others stayed by their men.'

The Collyer family were hoping to start a new life on an Idaho farm. Charlotte was reluctant in the extreme to leave her husband Harvey, but entered the boat with her eight-year-old daughter Marjorie just before it was too late. 'The deck seemed to be slipping under my feet,' she said.

It was leaning at a sharp angle; for the ship was then sinking fast, bows down. I clung desperately to my husband. I do not know what I said; but I shall always be glad to think that I did not want to leave him. A man seized me by the arm. Then another threw both his arms about my waist and dragged me away by main strength. I heard my husband say: 'Go, Lotty! For God's sake,

be brave, and go! I'll get a seat in another boat.' The men who
held me rushed me across the deck, and hurled me bodily into
the lifeboat.

She landed heavily on her shoulder and bruised it badly, and behind
her more women were crowding into 14. She stumbled to her feet
and, looking up on the boat deck, caught one last glimpse of her
husband's back as he disappeared in the crowd. 'His face was turned
away, so that I never saw it again.'[53]

Thomas Threlfall, the leading stoker who had worked below with
his men drawing fires, had been ordered up on deck about 1.20 a.m.
Fortunately for him, Lowe needed more crew for rowing and he
was directed into 14. Another fortunate to make it was Alfred Pugh,
a twenty-one-year-old steward. His brother, a leading fireman, went
down with the ship.

Lowe asked Scarrott how many were in the boat and received the
reply that there were fifty-four women and four children. Although
Boat 14 was below capacity, some felt it was overfilled. Passenger Eva
Hart later described it as 'hopelessly overcrowded'. As far as Lowe
was concerned, she was loaded with as many as she could take.

He turned to his colleague, Sixth Officer James Moody, who was
busy with Boat 16. Several boats had gone without an officer, he said,
and a 'responsible person' was needed in each. Moody responded:
'You go. I will get away in some other boat.' Lowe responded: 'All
right, you go in that boat and I will go in this.'

To what degree self-preservation motivated Lowe in this action
can only be speculated upon; no doubt the instinct for survival was
highly developed, but so too was a devotion to duty and sense of
personal honour. Did any of the senior officers know that Lowe was
leaving in command of a lifeboat? Chief Officer Wilde was working in this area and may have approved the departure. AB Frederick
Clench stated that, 'We had instructions when we went down that
we were to keep our eye on No. 14 boat, where Mr. Lowe, the fifth
officer, was, and keep all together as much as we could, so that we
would not get drifted away from one another.' Although he does not
say who these orders came from, it was Wilde who ordered him into
the boat. Clench's testimony also makes it clear that the plan to keep
the boats together was formulated before they had left the boat decks.

As they began lowering 14, at least two desperate men decided to
take a chance, armed officer or no, and hurtled through the air, into

the boat. Lowe physically hauled one of them from the benches and deposited him on deck. The other was to receive different treatment.

Charlotte Collyer recalled, 'a young lad, hardly more than a schoolboy, pink-cheeked, almost small enough to be counted as a child.' A possible candidate is Joseph Nicholls, nineteen, who had earlier helped his mother and younger half-brother into 14 and asked permission to join them. His mother said he was refused, and told he would be shot if he attempted to do so.

Whoever he was, the would-be stowaway attempted to hide in the bottom of the boat. Lowe was ruthless. Hunting him down, he stuck the Browning automatic in the youth's face. 'I give you just ten seconds to get back on to that ship before I blow your brains out!'

The boarder was too terrified to move. Lowe put the gun aside and appealed to his sense of honour. 'For God's sake, be a man!' he hissed. 'We've got women and children to save. We must stop at the decks lower down and take on women and children.' The weeping youth began to comply. At this point young Marjorie Collyer spoke up, taking Lowe's hand. 'Oh, Mr Man, don't shoot, please don't shoot the poor man!' [54]

Lowe later declared he would never forget the child's plea. He smiled down reassuringly down at her as the entrant crept back on deck. The body of Joseph Nicholls was later recovered, only to be buried at sea.

Officer Lowe would allow no more jumpers. 'We want no dirty work here,' he told the crew. 'I'll shoot two at a time.' [55] As they lowered from the Boat Deck to A Deck, a press of steerage men lined the rail, gaunt terror making them appear threatening to those in the lifeboat. To Lowe and others, their views tinted by the prejudice of their age, these men were 'Italian' in appearance; a very unlikely conclusion, particularly given the comparatively low numbers of Italian passengers on board.

As they looked set to 'spring in', Lowe extended his gun at arm's length. He fired a warning shot – splitting the night – to scare them off. He did the same at each successive deck, the shots directed along the ship's side. Clear Cameron said he cried, 'If any one of you men jump into this boat, I will shoot you like the dogs you are. So stand back!' [56]

Daisy Minahan claimed that, 'As we reached the level of each deck, men jumped into the boat – until the officer threatened to shoot the next man who jumped.' Survivor Edith Brown vividly

remembered Lowe telling one leaper: 'You could have capsized the
boat! I've got a good mind to shoot you!' As a consequence, Boat 14
did not stop at any deck to take on more passengers.[57]

Boat 14 still had one more problem to overcome before reaching
the water. It had been an uneven descent, with passengers fearing
that they might be pitched into the sea by the jerking of the falls.
Finally, while still several feet above the surface of the water, the
tackle completely jammed. So near, and yet so far.

Scarrott thought that the after-fall was twisted, but Lowe, looking up, could not see the cause. He opted to drop the remaining
distance, telling a crewman to stand by to release the boat from its
ropes. On his command the boat was 'slipped' and Boat 14 smacked
to the sea.

When they had all regained their composure after a fountain of
spray, Lowe ordered them to pull away. He immediately set about
organising the lifeboat, insisting on having the mast raised, and
crawling forward to see to it himself. After returning to his place,
he instructed men who had tobacco to keep it in their pockets –
'tobacco makes you thirsty.' He also ordered them to turn over all
their matches to him; these would become increasingly important
the longer they were in the open boats.

They remained close to the dying enormity. Lowe's initial idea
was to stay as near as possible, but he bowed to pressure from the
passengers and agreed to stand off, saying, 'I don't like to leave her,
but if you feel that way about it we will pull away a little distance.'
He instructed the men not to pull far.[59]

As they rowed away, he asked Seaman Fred Crowe for the number
of people in the boat. As Crowe interpreted it, the officer intended
to pick up anyone coming over the side into the water. Bathroom
steward Frank Morris heard Lowe ask again how many were in the
boat and then opine that it was under-filled. They would have to
pull back for a rescue effort. The ship had not yet sunk, but Lowe
knew that those still aboard the *Titanic* would soon be struggling for
their lives.

After the misadventures of launching and immediate organisation, Lowe was able to put into action the plan to keep the boats
together. About 150 yards away from the sinking ship he joined up
with boats 10 and 12, which up to then had been under the command of John Poingdestre.

Lowe began to look towards rounding up any other boats he could, telling those without an officer to 'consider yourself under my charge'. By his own account he 'returned and escorted another boat to the other two,' then sought out yet another one and took it to the three already assembled. Evidence on Lowe's flotilla – as on so many other points – is confused. While Clench in Boat 12 knew they were under Lowe's command, Buley in Boat 10 would recall Lowe's reaching his and Poingdestre's boat an hour after they left the *Titanic's* side.

Lowe eventually corralled five boats, with scores of occupants each. Many individuals would testify at the subsequent inquiries or relate their accounts in the media or private correspondence, with all the contradictions and confusion to be expected from such a kaleidoscope.

It is evident that Lowe's primary concern was to take charge of as many boats as possible. At the same time, everyone else was focused on the impending end of a mammoth liner. The internal stresses in the *Titanic* howled her agony to every ear as the screams of the doomed piled higher. At the very end it seemed to Harold Lowe that she assumed an angle of 75 degrees. The lifeboats watched as rows of portholes, 'long ribbons of light against a great black shape,' slid sickeningly from view. While Lowe appeared to believe that she sank intact, others witnessed a horrendous rending and screeching of metal.[60]

Clear Cameron believed she saw the ship break in two. Lowe heard 'a kind of distant smothered rumbling' as the *Titanic* went under. The maiden voyage had ended in a nosedive, over 960 miles from New York.

CHAPTER 9

'I'VE TAKEN
COMMAND HERE'

From one boat to the next, the cries from the drowning prompted debate about returning. They ranged from half-hearted suggestions and desultory comments to open demands that were shouted down by others. When the subject came up in Boat 1, Lady Duff Gordon evoked the spectre of swamping, a fear common to crew and passengers alike. There was no more talk of returning.

In Boat 6, the passengers wanted to go back. Some women urged Quartermaster Robert Hichens to turn the boat around. Fellow occupant Major Arthur Peuchen told them, 'It's no use you arguing with that man at all. It is best not to discuss matters with him.' Hichens, who had talked of 'our lives, not theirs', now said it was no use going back, that there were 'only a lot of stiffs there.'

In Boat 8, crewman Thomas Jones wanted to return. He had hesitated on reaching the water and stood by for some time, hoping to be of assistance, but the women had protested that he should get the boat away. The Countess of Rothes remembered how torn Jones was over the decision.

Albert Haines in Boat 9 conferred with the crew in his boat. 'There are people in the water,' he pointed out. Was it advisable to go back? 'We can't do nothing with this crowd we have in the boat' he eventually decided.

Fourth Officer Boxhall was in an unhappy predicament. Ordered to take command of No.2 lifeboat, he had left the ship quite late. He had insufficient crew, with only one man adequately understanding his orders. Nonetheless he attempted to obey instructions he had been given to take the boat to the gangway doors until he became alarmed by suction as the great hull settled.

He decided to pull off some distance. There he stood by, unaware that there was comparatively little suction when the ship at last went under. He did not return for survivors after the ship went down, but lit the first of a number of flares he had taken with him into the boat. A chorus of screams from the water momentarily swelled at the sudden signal, only to die down again.

For a moment it seemed as if Boat 5, under the command of Officer Pitman, would take the initiative in a rescue attempt. 'Now, men, we will pull toward the wreck,' he ordered, and turned the boat towards the struggling mass. The crew edged a little distance toward the swimmers, but a storm of protest arose from Boat 5's passengers. They told him that it was a mad idea. If he was to go among the victims the boat would be swamped, and they would merely add themselves to the catalogue of drowned. Pitman, in a choice that was to haunt him, changed his mind. They took in their oars and 'simply lay there doing nothing' as the 'continual moan', strong at first, ebbed to silence.[61]

Lifeboat 4 left the ship under the charge of Quartermaster Walter Perkis, supported by AB William McCarthy and Storekeeper John 'Jack' Foley. Late in launching, she remained in fairly close proximity to the ship. At least one crewman, seeing her from the decks of the liner, was able to swim to the boat before the *Titanic* went down. After the ship sank, Boat 4 was close enough for others to make their way to her and for the crew of the boat to row back and pick up survivors. The evidence concerning Boat 4 is somewhat ambiguous, both among those in the water and those in the boat. Although some of those in the small craft resisted the idea of rescue efforts, others persisted in their desire to return. Some in the water swam towards Boat 4, some were met by the boat part way and others were sought out in the wreckage. Before long, Boat 4 also pulled away from the mass of people in the water.

After the ship had sunk, Emily Ryerson in Boat 4 was to recall that there were no lights to be seen, and 'no one seemed to know what direction to take'.[62] In the darkness they heard Lowe, who had earlier called out to them to tie up to his boats, blowing his whistle to corral the other vessels. Once their eyesight adjusted to the darkness, following Lowe's voice, Boat 4 was able to tie up with Boat 14.

Lowe's initial impulse seems to have been to return his entire flotilla to the scene of the wreck. According to Crowe this met with a very lukewarm reception. 'The ladies seemed to make a protest at his idea of going back.' After tying up the boats, Lowe had his men ship their oars while he waited for the cries to subside. He was prepared to pick up anyone who managed to swim out of the general tangle, but not to risk a return with over 1,000 people thrashing for their lives.[63]

'It would have been suicide' to go back, he said later, at least until the people in the water had 'thinned out'.

He added, 'What are you going to do with a boat of 65 where 1,600 people are drowning?' AB George Moore, who left the ship in Boat 3, observed: 'Five or six pulling on a boat's gunwales would no doubt have capsized the boat.'

The cries were terrible. They seemed, one crewman in Boat 14 said, to 'go through you like a knife'. How long they waited is a matter for speculation. Lowe felt it was an hour.

Daisy Minahan noted that in the meantime Lowe suggested that a good song to sing would be 'Throw Out the Lifeline'. She did not indicate whether the words were in earnest or said with sarcasm or in an attempt at black humour. The grim remark may have been sparked by the sound of singing from some other boats, with one woman out on the water leading the hymn 'Eternal Father, Strong to Save'.

'Throw out the Lifeline' was, as it happens, singularly appropriate to the situation. Written in 1888 by Edwin Ufford after observing a lifeboat drill near Boston, it runs in part:

> Throw out the life line, across the dark wave;
> There is a brother whom someone should save;
> Somebody's brother! O who then will dare
> To throw out the life line, his peril to share?

> Throw out the life line with hand quick and strong:
> Why do you tarry, why linger so long?
> See! he is sinking; oh, hasten today
> And out with the life boat! away, then away!

The suggestion of a song was not the only comment that caused Miss Minahan consternation. Equally dire in her view was Lowe's next remark that, 'I think the best thing for you women to do is to take a nap.' Some of the ladies requested that Lowe return for survivors, she added. His alleged response was: 'You ought to be damn glad you are here and have got your own life.'

Lowe's comments, as she recorded them, give the impression of a man as cold as some felt Hichens was. Yet other survivors would claim that Lowe had expressed the desire to return some considerable time prior to doing so. Even before the ship sank, according to one of Boat 14's crew, he stated, 'Well, boys, I am prepared to row nearer and take my chance. I don't think there's any fear of being sucked down. Are the rest prepared to go?' They were not.[64]

Clear Cameron said: 'He wanted to go back and try to help some of the drowning but we begged and implored him not to as we were full and we should all be drowned, so he didn't for some time.'[65]

Daisy Minahan found Lowe's language confrontational. 'He had been so blasphemous during the two hours we were in his boat that the women at my end of the boat all thought he was under the influence of liquor,' she wrote. Blasphemy in this context appears to centre on the word 'damn', a mild epithet today.[66]

But to others in the boats, Lowe represented the leader that the situation called for. Rene Harris was one of the occupants of Collapsible D. She was distraught at having lost her husband. Her initial awareness of Lowe was as a voice that called encouragement out of the darkness. 'Everybody happy?' 'You're tied fast. Don't worry.' At intervals he called out, 'Any other boats around? Tie up to me.'[67]

The very vigour of the language that so disgusted Minahan had its appeal elsewhere. 'He is a proper John Bull, cares for no one and he is quite young' enthused Clear Cameron, while Sarah Compton, whose brother's entry to the boats had been blocked by Lowe, wrote of the 'manly bearing' that inspired confidence, and how he personified 'the best traditions of the British sailor.' Edith Brown, herself only fifteen, referred to him ever after as a 'brave young man'.[68]

Boat 14, meanwhile, had another problem to contend with. It had sprung a leak, possibly from dropping while being lowered. One of the women shouted that water was coming up over her ankles, and the bails kept in the lifeboat were frantically put to use. As they waited, Lowe had the opportunity to again observe the lights of the mystery ship that appeared so close. As he watched she seemed to alter her position and make visible her green starboard light instead of the red. Then 'a few minutes afterwards all the lights went out.' With them extinguished all hope of prompt rescue until arrival of the *Carpathia* with the dawn.[69]

The volume of cries had dramatically reduced, indicating that the cold had killed or incapacitated most of those in the water. Lowe decided to transfer the passengers out of Boat 14 to give himself a clear boat to go back to the site of the sinking. This would also circumvent the protests of those women who did not wish to return. He impressed on his select crew what they were about to undertake, and began distributing the passengers out of Boat 14 to the others under his command.

Tying up the boats had been complicated enough, but shifting passengers proved to be far worse. It would have been difficult under the best of conditions, but now, with traumatised women and children in the dark of the middle Atlantic, Lowe found the work incredibly difficult. Time was running out, much quicker than he had evidently anticipated, the cries rapidly dying away. And Daisy Minahan was apparently not moving fast enough to suit him after her turn came. Lowe's temper snapped. 'Jump, God damn you, jump!' Miss Minahan, a first-class passenger after all, was deeply indignant.

One of the *Titanic* story's most striking incidents now occurred. While transferring passengers Lowe suddenly found an 'Italian'. who 'had a shawl over his head, and I suppose he had skirts.' Lowe pulled the headgear away to look at the face of a man who 'was in a great hurry to get into the other boat.' He contemptuously pitched him into the neighbouring craft, uttering not a single word to the stowaway.

Who this man was is unresolved. Several candidates have been suggested, including Irishman Eddie Ryan. He admitted freely in a letter to his parents in May 1912 that he had thrown a towel over his head, letting it hang down behind, before walking 'very stiff' past the officers barring the men from the aft boats on the port side.

Meanwhile there is the question of whether Lowe moved absolutely all his passengers out of Boat 14. He said he returned with 'an empty boat, just a boat's crew and no passengers.' Yet two passengers claim to have been in the boat when it returned, being Edith Haisman and Charlotte Collyer.

Others support Lowe's version of events. 'It was only manned by a crew,' said Quartermaster Bright, while Frank Morris agreed that 'we transferred all the women and children… I suppose this was Officer Lowe's idea: if we rowed back to the wreckage and picked up a lot, our boat would not hold them all. That was his idea, to save as many as possible.'

Collyer's story, given to the *Semi-Monthly Magazine* in May 1912, has long stood as one of the most cited passenger accounts of the events in Boat 14. Her story reads as a first-hand account of events in the boat as it returned to the scene of the wreck. But the events she describes (the rescue of men off an overturned lifeboat, the need for women to assist in rowing miles to the *Carpathia*) happened not to the occupants of Boat 14, but to those women who were switched from it to Boats 10 and 12. Her account is also contradicted by her daughter, Marjorie, who referred in her own newspaper interview to the officer's departure and return to the wreck in another boat.

Among the crew Lowe now hastily assembled was a second-class passenger who volunteered to assist. He was Charles Williams of Harrow, a champion squash player. Others included Crowe, Scarrott, Morris, Threlfall and Evans. Together they set off for the disaster site.

There were a few minutes of confusion over which direction to go. Lowe and his men had become disorientated while circling and rounding up other boats. Finally their ears reached a consensus and they found their way back by following the few faint calls that remained.

It was not always easy to distinguish between the wreckage and the bodies, but it was apparent that there were many of the latter – so many, said Evans, that 'you couldn't hardly count them.' He feared that if he looked over the side of Boat 14 his nerve would give way. It was very rapidly apparent to the would-be rescuers that the majority of people had frozen rather than drowned. They bobbed listlessly, head and shoulders supported by thick cork lifejackets. The faces either hung forward over the water or gazed sightlessly up at the stars. It was obvious that for the vast majority the lapse of time had proved conclusive.

There were, however, some that lived in the waste. The first man picked up was William Hoyt of New York. From what Lowe later told Hoyt's family, it would seem his attention was drawn to the first-class passenger by a moaning noise he was making. Hoyt may have been barely conscious. A large man weighed down by thoroughly soaked clothes, it was a gargantuan task to pull him into the lifeboat. Once there, Hoyt was found to be bleeding from the mouth and nose. Lowe propped him up in the stern and tried to revive him, removing his collar and loosening his shirt. But for Hoyt it was too late. He quickly expired.

They followed the moans further into the wreckage. This time they found a steward and wrenched him over the gunwale into the slatted sanctuary. Very cold, with his hands noticeably stiffened, the man managed to live until rescue arrived in the morning.

'You could not row, because of the bodies,' Lowe described. 'You had to push your way through.' They saw one man kneeling as if in prayer on what seemed to be a staircase. Although comparatively close, it was only with great difficulty that they got within reach on an oar to pull him to the boat.

Collyer gave a highly coloured version of this rescue. 'A little further on, we saw a floating door that must have been torn loose when the ship went down. Lying upon it, face downward, was a small Japanese. As far as we could see, he was dead.' With the sea washing over him, frozen stiff, he didn't answer when he was hailed. Collyer said Lowe hesitated over saving him, declaring 'What's the use? He's dead, likely, and if he isn't there's others better worth saving than a Jap!' As Collyer told it, Lowe had turned the boat around but changed his mind and went back to take the man on board. The women chafed the victim's hands and rubbed his feet, whereupon he opened his eyes and attempted to speak. Seeing his words were unintelligible to those around him, he 'struggled to his feet, stretched his arms above his head, and in five minutes or so had almost recovered his strength.

'One of the sailors near to him was so tired that he could hardly pull his oar. The Japanese bustled over, pushed him from his seat, took the oar and worked like a hero until we were finally picked up.' Lowe gaped in 'open mouthed surprise' and said: 'By Jove! I'm ashamed of what I said about the little blighter. I'd save the likes o' him six times over, if I got the chance.'[70]

While the story fitted the style of popular magazines, it presents several problems. There was only one Japanese passenger aboard, Masabumi Hosono, and he was saved by entering a lifeboat on deck. That an Asian passenger was saved was confirmed, however, by Clench, who remembered 'a Japanese or Chinese young fellow' that was picked up from wreckage.

Probably it was one of the eight sailors from Hong Kong, third-class passengers travelling to America to join a Donaldson Line ship. Five of these managed to find their way into a lifeboat, only to be later accused of having stowed away.

More critically for Charlotte Collyer's account, the women who rubbed the Asian's hands and feet were almost certainly not in Boat 14 when it went back. So what of her account of Lowe's language? While appearing to chime with his remarks about 'Italians' glaring like wild beasts as Boat 14 lowered, the refusal to initially rescue an

Asian passenger does not fit with Lowe's high regard for the Chinese from his Blue Funnel days.

Lowe disagreed with many of his peers who stereotyped them as lazy and devious. If he was close enough to be able to identify the ethnicity of an individual on a black sea, it must seem unlikely that he would not go that bit further to haul the victim aboard. This is, after all, a man who was reported to have once risked his own life by jumping overboard to save a Chinese man who had fallen from a ship underway.

Confusion exists as to how many Boat 14 rescued. Four is the most commonly cited number in evidence, a figure that includes Hoyt, who did not long survive after being pulled from the water. Probably not all of those the boat passed in the water were dead, but the crew had no way of determining.

Lowe noted that they saw no women. Of those few who had survived to be rescued, at least two had managed to support themselves on floating debris. But it was now apparent that there would be no more survivors. With the wind and sea picking up, Lowe raised the sail and they drew away to the other lifeboats. Scarrott recorded: 'As we left that awful scene we gave way to tears. It was enough to break the stoutest heart.'[71]

The dawn light fringed the horizon at 4 a.m. and with it the beauty of surrounding icebergs was revealed. 'If it hadn't been for the disaster,' thought Clear Cameron, transferred to Boat 10, 'the sight would have been splendid.'[72]

Lowe spotted Collapsible D, wallowing in the slopping waves. 'She was in pretty bad condition, because a breeze had sprung up and there was some sea, and she was somewhat overcrowded.' D was finding it difficult to make any headway as she had few crew.

'How are you?' he hailed. First-class passenger Hugh Woolner shouted back, 'We have about all we want!' apparently fearful that Lowe might want to load more people into their boat. 'Would you like a tow?' asked the officer. The response was rapturous.

At length the shape of the *Carpathia*, responding to the *Titanic*'s distress signals, became visible. 'Call to her,' advised one. 'Wait for her to come after us. Don't go near the ice,' said another. Lowe did not welcome the input. 'I've taken command here,' he said sternly. 'I intend to keep command because no one else seems to have sense enough to do it. Now, shut up. We will go to the boat. We can't expect her to come to us.'[73]

Unspoken, the thought passed through his mind that the *Carpathia* might not have sighted them in the semi-gloom. But while 'bowling along very nicely' at 4 or 5 knots in the breeze, Lowe caught sight of another craft that seemed in difficulties. Those aboard were shouting for assistance.

'There's a boat ahead. It's almost under,' he yelled to his crew.

As he approached he fired four shots from his Browning into the water. These were interpreted as a signal by some, but more thought it a warning not to swamp the boat as he drew alongside. According to Evans, Lowe said it was the latter.

Both Collapsible A and its occupants were in poor condition. The boat had been thrown clear of the *Titanic* after efforts to launch it were overwhelmed by the final plunge. It had remained right-side up, and although damaged and waterlogged, was a refuge for swimmers.

As horrific as the night's events had been for the crew of Boat 14, it was minor compared to the experiences suffered by those who made it to Collapsible A. When passenger George Rheims got there, those inside had at first refused to let him enter. While he scrambled in, others had not been so fortunate. 'We had to push back about 10 poor people who wanted to climb aboard. We were filled to the limit,' he said. [74]

The survivors stood, balancing their weight in order to prevent a capsize. Rheims shivered severely in his underwear, twice considering throwing himself into the ocean in order to bring an end to the agony. Only the thought of his wife ashore held him back.

Lowe shouted a warning as he approached. According to Mrs Harris, it was: 'The woman first. I will shoot the man who tries to get ahead.' He swung the slight form of Rhoda Abbott, the sole female occupant, into the boat, where she drooped brokenly. The others followed aboard, warned by Lowe, 'One man at a time. Death to the man who makes a rush.'[75]

Three forms remained lying in the bottom of the collapsible. Lowe asked the others if they were sure the three, all men, were dead. 'Absolutely sure,' came the response. Lowe decided to leave the corpses. 'I am not here to worry about bodies,' he rationalised, 'I am here for life, to save life, and not to bother about bodies.'

He shoved off from the raft, fully expecting her to sink with her grisly load. Ironically, she perhaps deserved the appellation 'unsinkable' more than the *Titanic*. Collapsible A, which looked as if she would go down at any moment, was found the following month by the crew of the *Oceanic*. The bodies were still aboard and were buried at sea.

Some dozen people were taken from A. One of the women in D produced a flask of whisky that was passed first to Abbott and then to the others. Rescue was close at hand now, and Lowe made for their salvation. A sequence of photos taken on the *Carpathia* shows the approach of Boat 14 under sail – Lowe at the tiller – with D in tow.

As he approached, Lowe reefed sail and urged his men to the oars. One who responded was Steward Edward Brown, recently saved from A. Although his feet had swollen so that they had 'burst' his boots, with his hands similarly distended, Brown gamely took an oar.

They were hoisted aboard at 6am. As the passengers and crew were lifted in succession, followed by Hoyt's body, Lowe busied himself stowing the gear. It was a pointless exercise, if instinctive. Boat 14 was one of the lifeboats set adrift rather than taken aboard *Carpathia*.

Asked later what he did after landing his human cargo, Lowe responded: 'There was nothing to do.' A sense of desolation was in his follow-up question: 'What was there to do?'[76]

CHAPTER 10

THE US TITANIC INQUIRY

The *Carpathia* crept through a thunderstorm to her pier in New York. Among those waiting for the press-dubbed 'Ship of Widows' was Senator William Alden Smith of Wisconsin. Smith was about to chair the hearings of the US Senate Subcommittee of Commerce into the disaster.

Accompanying Smith as he boarded the *Carpathia* was Joe Bayliss, Sheriff of Chippewa County, Michigan, whom Smith had seized upon as the ideal man to undertake the tricky job of delivering sub-poenas and eliciting information.

Much was unobtainable: Captain Smith, Chief Officer Wilde and First Officer Murdoch, key men from the time of the collision to managing its aftermath, had all been swept away. Second Officer Lightoller was the most senior crew survivor, followed by junior officers Pitman, Boxhall and Lowe. Of the juniors, only one – Moody – had perished. He had not gone in another boat as he had told Lowe he intended to do, staying instead with the sinking ship and trying to launch the last of the collapsible boats as the *Titanic* sank from under him. Lowe had known no one aboard prior to his arrival in Belfast, but many of the *Titanic*'s crew had lost friends and colleagues they had known for years. Lightoller, who had served with the line the longest of the surviving officers, lost many friends – including William Murdoch, whom he had first served with on the Australia run many years beforehand, journeying on the *Medic* down to the Southern hemisphere.

The press, out of touch with the *Carpathia* for three days, had been rife with rumour and sensation. On the *Carpathia* itself, the pain-ful completion of the *Titanic*'s maiden voyage had generated its own stories. Certainly the surviving officers had time to get theirs straight.

Lowe also had an opportunity to mingle with those he had res-cued. 'I would go around and see – well, I don't know. I suppose you might deem them your friends; I suppose you could,' he said. 'They were very suddenly brought together, and all that. I used to go around among them; and I knew my boat crew.'[77]

Of those whom Boat 14 had pulled from the water, however, he heard nothing. None later approached to speak with the man who had saved their lives. The body of William F. Hoyt was among those buried at sea from the Cunarder.

One who did approach Lowe was a first-class American survivor who indicated that he wanted to exchange souvenirs. He pulled some gold sovereigns from his pocket. 'You had better have one of these, they will be no good to me in America,' he smiled. Lowe replied 'Well, if you want a souvenir, you can have the bullet you nearly got.'[78]

The newspapers had been full of shootings and suicides and now the Americans wanted to find out the truth. For Sheriff Bayliss, 'kidnapped for a few days' by Senator Smith, the next few days were to prove the most eventful of his life to date.

J. Bruce Ismay, the managing director of the White Star Line, berated at Lifeboat 5 by Harold Lowe, was already a prime target. Ismay had survived in controversial circumstances – entering a lifeboat while many of his paying customers, men especially, had to stand back and die. He had later shut himself away on the *Carpathia*, planning only to hold a company vessel at New York for a quick return to England. Now his cabin was entered and Ismay was served with legal papers. Bayliss also forced subpoenas on many members of the crew, including all the living officers. The return to families and loved ones would be perforce delayed.

When he called at a hotel to serve the papers on the young wireless operator of the *Carpathia*, Harold Cottam protested that he hadn't even been aboard the *Titanic*, that they had no right to interfere with him and he would not comply. Bayliss 'told him to keep quiet or I would take him up and put him under my bed and later see that he got there all right.'[79]

As Smith opened his Inquiry the following day, Bayliss was organising interviews with the crew. By midnight he was able to present Smith with a list of twenty-nine crewmen in addition to those already subpoenaed whom he felt had important information. One was Quartermaster Robert Hichens, the man reluctant to return for a 'lot of stiffs.' His departure from New York aboard the *Lapland* was intercepted by tugboat, and Hichens was forced to return.

The crew already knew that they would have to face a Board of Trade Inquiry in Britain – mandatory for every marine casualty – but the idea of having to face an American one as well was unprecedented. Bayliss found the crew as a whole surly and uncooperative.

Lowe was there as Smith called his first witnesses in the Waldorf-Astoria Hotel on Friday 19 April. He listened attentively as Lightoller followed Ismay in evidence. The second officer was already stone-walling. 'It was hard to dig anything out of him,' commented *The New York Times*. He was 'short and abrupt.'

Lowe had been anything but on the *Carpathia*. Guileless as ever, he had not tried to play down his gunfire during the evacuation, displaying for American first-class passenger Margaret Brown the Browning he had used to enforce his commands on the boat deck and while lowering.

Brown, later immortalised as 'The Unsinkable Molly Brown', heard Lowe tell her that he had his fellow officers had seen to it that the saved would not include 'any of the rich nabobs'. Brown thought him 'preening his feathers' over the fact, although he did express one regret – the language he had used to women like Minahan in the boats. [80]

Such stories were now being assiduously gathered by Bayliss and his investigators. Meanwhile it appeared that the fifth officer had left the sinking ship without orders to do so. There was a risk he could yet be accused of cowardice… although he was fortunate in the numbers coming forward spontaneously to speak of their admiration for his actions.

One of the earliest testimonials appeared in a Reuters telegram, dated the day after *Carpathia*'s return to New York and published on both sides of the Atlantic:

A young Englishwoman, who requested that her name might be omitted, told a story of her experience on one of the collapsible boats which was manned by eight of the crew and commanded by Mr. Lowe, whose actions she described as having saved the lives of many before the boat was launched.

Mr Lowe passed along the deck of the *Titanic* commanding people not to jump into the boats and otherwise restraining them from swamping the craft. When the collapsible boat was launched he succeeded in putting up a mast and sail. He collected other boats, and in some cases where the boats were short of adequate crew, he made an exchange, whereby each was properly manned.

Mr Lowe threw lines to connect the boats two by two so that all moved together. Later he went back to the wreck. One boat succeeded in picking up some of those who had jumped overboard and who were swimming about. On his way back to the *Carpathia* he passed one of the collapsible boats which was on the point of sinking with thirty persons on board, most of them in scant night clothing. They were rescued in the nick of time.

Clear Cameron, who did not give interviews, expressed her views privately in a letter written two days later in which she described Lowe's pistol shots – 'and thankful we were, for as we got down level with the first deck there were a lot of the immigrant men just ready to spring into our boat, which was already full.' Her admiration for him was infused with patriotic pride; several times in letters she referred to Lowe as a real 'John Bull', adding that he was the only officer who did any work. 'We people who were saved in the last four boats owe our lives to him.'[81]

It was a view shared by second-class passenger Selena Cook, who told the *Cleveland Plain Dealer*: 'Too much praise cannot be given the officer for his work,' she enthused, adding to the *Daily Telegram*, 'with fifty-four other women on board the *Titanic*, I owe my life to Mr Harold G. Lowe.'

The crew had opinions too. Frank Morris was to be asked directly whether the crew of Boat 14 had made every possible effort. Morris answered, 'Our officer did the finest action he could have done.' Thomas Threlfall, in what the newspapers described as 'burst of genuine feeling' declared him to be 'a gentleman and a Britisher.'[82]

Bayliss gave Lowe his summons on 20 April, informing him that he was to present himself in Washington DC, the city to which the Inquiry was moving, by Monday 22 April. Chairman, committee and witnesses all travelled by train, the crew in a special coach under the watchful eye of Bayliss.

During the journey Bayliss and Lowe fell into conversation. The two men soon discovered they had much in common, and despite their opposing perspectives, a friendship began to evolve. It continued to develop once they arrived, despite an early argument between officialdom and the *Titanic's* officers.

All officers and crew were to be housed in the Continental Hotel, an arrangement that annoyed Lightoller. The senior surviving officer wanted the higher ranks quartered other than with the men in a 'second-rate boarding house.'

Bill McKinstry, secretary to Senator Smith, exclaimed to Lightoller in response, 'My God! Your captain now sleeps quartered with the crew under the waves!' The issue was finally resolved when the officers were given their own floor and separate dining arrangements. They would, however, move hotels again before the inquiry was through with them.

Lowe had meanwhile learned little about keeping his own counsel. As Lightoller grappled with officialdom, Harold Lowe confronted the reporters for whom he had already developed an intense distaste. Stories that had appeared claiming the crew were being kept under guard outraged him, as had the attempts by the press to photograph him and his colleagues in New York with their 'dirty cameras'. Now, he had a chance to set the record straight with the reporter from the *Washington Post*. 'We have been placed under no injunctions to keep still,' he declared with some defiance. 'We all welcome this inquiry. But you Americans got up against us, and now we Britishers are up against you, and we shall see how it comes out.' While his view might have been representative of the real sentiments of the officers and probably not a few of the crew, this adversarial take on trans-Atlantic relations did not accord with the official White Star line stressing full co-operation with the inquiry. Those reporters who had tried to get a list of officers and crew registered at the Continental came in for special mention. 'In England, I say a man would get a punch in the nose if he attempted to look over the guest book.' In such a frame of mind he prepared to give evidence.

He could not have anticipated an easy time on the witness stand. Officer Pitman had been subjected to a pitiless line of questioning on his failure to return for survivors until he broke down in tears. Neither Lightoller nor Boxhall had fared much better. Boxhall, afflicted with chest pains since the disaster, had been placed under medical care after one day's testimony, was diagnosed as suffering from pleurisy.

On Wednesday 24 April, Senator Smith intoned, 'I would like to call Mr Lowe, the Fifth Officer.' Lowe was sworn, gave his name and was then told, 'I would like to have you turn your chair so that you are facing the reporter.'

'I am facing you, sir.'

'Turn your chair so you will look directly at the reporter.'

The interaction between senator and sailor had not got off to an auspicious beginning. It would soon deteriorate. In response to a question about *Titanic*'s sea trials, he blithely replied, 'I could no more tell you now than fly.' Smith suggested the date of the trials was 2 April, and Lowe responded, 'I do not know, Sir. I suppose it would be if you say so.'

'Well, look it up yourself,' the senator said. 'You are testifying. I am not testifying.'

'We do not get any notice of these things –'

'I am not criticising you –'

'We have not started our voyage yet.'

'I am not criticising you. I simply want to know when you first saw this ship.'[83]

The developing tension between the two men was to become an outstanding characteristic of Lowe's evidence. Like his fellow officers and many of the crew, Lowe resented the fact that he was expected to give evidence in America at all.

Smith's repetitive questioning, coupled with a general ignorance of all matters maritime, was more than enough to irritate, and there is an undeniable truculence to many of Lowe's responses.

They moved from sea trials to departure. The weather was pleasant when the ship left Southampton, Lowe confirmed, adding, 'I should say it was about 48.'

'Above zero?' blurted the chairman.

Lowe bristled. 'Forty-eight degrees Fahrenheit,' he enunciated. His irritation was evident to the reporters. 'Frequent tilts between Lowe and Smith enlivened the proceedings,' one paper asserted.

Next some actual ice entered the relationship. Did Lowe know what proportion of an iceberg was supposed to be submerged? One-eighth, he seemed to recall. Where did he learn that? At school. From whence did they originate? Lowe knew of only two places.

'Name them,' Smith commanded. The polar regions, offered Lowe. 'The Arctic regions?' asked Smith and Lowe agreed. Now: 'Do you know what an iceberg is composed of?'

'Ice, I suppose, Sir.'

The raucous laughter in the Inquiry room echoed through the newspapers, as it has in books and articles since. Stung, Smith followed by asking if he had ever heard of icebergs composed not only of ice, but 'of rock and earth and other substances,' as had been testified by Boxhall. Lowe had not.

Matters soon built up to a fresh skirmish:

'Are you a temperate man?'

'I am, sir. I never touched it in my life. I am an abstainer.'

'I am very glad to have you say that.'

'I say it, sir, without fear of contradiction.'

'I am not contradicting you, and I congratulate you upon it; but so many stories have been circulated; one has just been passed up to me now, from a reputable man, who says it was reported that you were drinking that night.'

For Lowe, the son of an alcoholic, the charge was deeply felt.

'Me, Sir?' He leaned forward in his chair, his face flushing.

'That is the reason I asked the question.'

'No, Sir. This –' He held up his glass of water – 'is the strongest drink I ever take.' He was 'extremely angry and spoke the words with some heat,' the newspapers recorded.

Not all the exchanges reported in the newspapers appear in the transcript. Smith was known in some instances to tap the stenographer's hand when he wished something left out of the official record, as when Pitman broke down under questioning.

One heated exchange found only in press reports had Smith asking: 'You could say 'Go to hell' to Ismay, why can't you answer my questions?' Lowe retorted: 'I do answer them in my own best way. When I can understand them.' It was observed that 'Smith and Lowe constantly quibbled and became sarcastic.'

Evidence on the Ismay altercation provided Lowe with the opportunity to lash out afresh. Lowe said he had spoken as he did 'because Mr Ismay was overanxious and he was getting a trifle excited.' Ismay, managing director of the line, was sitting nearby, yet Lowe now waved his hand in imitation of Ismay's hand gestures as he said 'Lower away! Lower away! Lower away!'

'Give us what you said!' Ismay suddenly interrupted. Astonishingly, Lowe turned once more on his employer in full public view. 'The chairman is examining me,' he retorted. Now Senator Smith found himself the referee. He asked Ismay if he wanted Lowe to repeat the language used on the boat deck. 'I have no objection to his giving it,' answered Ismay. 'It was not very parliamentary.'

The words were first written down, to see if they would be uttered aloud in the presence of ladies. Smith decided that they could. Lowe then explained: 'I told him "If you will get to hell out of that, I shall be able to do something".'

Perhaps conscious that Ismay had already been to hell and back with the American press – or possibly more mindful of his own precarious position – Lowe now soothed: '… also, of course, he only did this because he was anxious to get the people away and so to help me.'

Lowe was providing great copy. At one point, when asked if he was aware of icebergs in the vicinity of the Grand Banks, the press gleefully noted that Lowe yawned. Yet it could have been real fatigue. Some sources suggest that Lowe was visibly affected when giving evidence, relating in a 'broken voice' the ghastly scenes as the ship sank and the sounds from the water that followed.

He was asked a series of questions about gunshots – 'I heard them, and I fired them,' said Lowe intriguingly – and explained:

> As we were coming down the decks, coming down past the open decks, I saw a lot of Italians, Latin people, all along the ship's rails – understand, it was open – and they were all glaring, more or less like wild beasts, ready to spring. That is why I yelled out to look out, and let go, bang, right along the ship's side.
>
> I fired these shots and without intention of hurting anybody and also with the knowledge that I did not hurt anybody. I am absolutely positive I hit nobody.

Public reaction to Lowe's testimony was predominantly favourable. A group of female students in the audience showed a schoolgirl appreciation of his looks and presence and he was not oblivious to the attention they paid him. Others, including representatives of the media, were almost as taken with him. 'From first to last Lowe's story showed that he played the man,' said the Omaha *World Herald*. Whatever Senator Smith himself thought of his jousts with Harold Lowe, his sheriff Joe Bayliss was also becoming an admirer.

Not only did Bayliss have access to Lowe, but also to Boat 14's other crew, having been detailed by Smith to spend time with *Titanic*'s personnel. Bayliss developed a respect for many, but reserved his highest commendation for the fifth officer.

'When the *Titanic* disaster has become a matter of history,' he wrote, 'Harold G. Lowe will occupy the hero's place.' Lowe combined qualities of courage, firmness and good judgement, he reasoned. While none of his fellow officers lacked courage, 'in this country at least, we honour most the man who gets results.'

Lowe's equilibrium in the face of plaudits, following coolness under intense scrutiny, was also noted by Smith's sheriff. He told Lowe: 'It was a source of wonder to me that you seemed to take all the important events with which you were connected just as a matter of ordinary procedure, and that the special praise handed out to you did not effect [*sic*] you in the least.'[84]

Yet there was something of a backlash. After Lowe and his fellow officers had left the country, Daisy Minahan went on the record with her recollections of how he had handled himself. Her affidavit, sworn on 13 May, showed the fifth officer in an 'unfortunate, bad light' as first-class survivor Archibald Gracie put it.

Although he hadn't seen Lowe's conduct during the evacuation, Gracie met him in Washington when both were giving evidence. He was also in touch with survivors during the compilation of his book, *The Truth About the Titanic*, published in 1913. Gracie's view was that Lowe was 'intemperate in his language only,' and 'in all other respects a first class officer.'

Sheriff Bayliss sent Lowe an editorial from the Michigan *Courier Herald*, saying it was 'intended as an answer to the attempted criticism of your conduct in swearing at some poor feminine creature who testified last week before the Senate.' Bayliss clearly felt a certain solidarity with sharp-tongued Lowe, and the editorial itself was scathing of Minahan's sensibilities, noting with heavy sarcasm that Lowe 'should have confined his choice of words to those that would have been appropriate in a friendly game of parlour croquet.'

The *Courier Herald* went on, 'As we look back on the stories of the sinking of the *Titanic* the figure of this man Lowe looms gigantic, masterful, above his fellows.' Bayliss added, 'You have reason to feel very proud of yourself… and thank God you have English blood enough to keep the plaudits of the multitude from turning your head.'

Others also stepped forward to answer Minahan's condemnation, among them Rhoda Abbott. Describing her harrowing experiences on Collapsible A to the *Providence Daily Journal*, she echoed the earlier words of Selena Rogers. 'Had it not been for Officer Lowe, I would have been drowned. I was nearly exhausted when he lifted me into his lifeboat. It would have been impossible for an officer to show more courtesy and many of the criticisms that have been made against this man are very unjust.'[85]

Another to come forward in his defence was a figure from Lowe's childhood, Shennie Lewis, now resident in the United States. Although ten years older than Lowe, she had known him when he was a boy in Barmouth. She wrote pointedly to the *New York Times* in May 1912 that 'whether the truth of the statement of his blasphemy exists or not, I should consider it trivial as compared to the positive knowledge of his courage and services described and proved at the Washington investigation.'

Lewis wrote that Lowe had once saved her brother's life at the risk of his own. As to Minahan's reference to Lowe being 'so blasphemous during the two hours we were in his boat that the women at my end all thought he was under the influence of liquor,' Lewis commented on the 'commonly known fact among his associates that he is, and always has been, a total abstainer.'

For Lowe, the allegation of intoxication rankled bitterly. Further reflection made him contemplate demanding to know from whom the charge had originated. Word of this filtered through to the newspapers and was duly reported. His concerns were practical as well as personal; as he explained to a reporter from *The World*, next to his master's ticket he valued most his reputation as an abstainer.

'It is a big part of a chap's value as a mariner, and I certainly trust that the readers of the newspapers both here and at home have not got a wrong idea from the testimony before these Senators,' he said. Lowe wrote to Smith seeking to have the issue put beyond all doubt, and considered pressing the matter even further. It took the combined efforts of friends and the counsel for the White Star Line to dissuade him from making more of the issue.

To reporters from *The World*, Senator Smith now backtracked by commenting that he was 'really glad that I had the chance to bring out the facts regarding this brave young officer,' and was 'perfectly satisfied' by Lowe's statement of sobriety.

The US Inquiry chairman also made an announcement before adjourning for lunch on 29 April, 'I desire to make a statement to go upon the record. In my examination of Officer Lowe the other day I asked him with reference to his habits [*sic*]. He informed me that he was a teetotaller. I accepted his statement as final, and congratulated him at that time. There is not the slightest disposition on the part of the committee to cast any reflection upon Mr. Lowe's habits. I think the difficulty arose of the statement of one of the witnesses, referring to his disposition rather than to his habits, and I am very glad to make that correction.'

Lowe spoke up from his seat at the back of the committee room. 'Thank you, Sir,' he said, adding, the newspapers recorded, 'I can go now.'

Lowe had the committee's blessing for his departure. During the afternoon session that day, members of crew were given permission to leave the United States. Lightoller departed almost immediately for New York, while Lowe and the other junior officers remained briefly in Washington to oversee final arrangements for the men.

Meanwhile Lowe had a correction of his own to make for inclusion in the official record. He had been approached by the Italian ambassador over his remarks about the 'Italians, Latin people' who were 'all glaring, more or less like wild beasts'. In the legal office of the Italian Embassy, Lowe drafted a statement retracting the description. The wording is unmistakably his own:

> I do hereby cancel the world 'Italian' and substitute the words 'immigrants belonging to Latin races.' In fact, I did not mean to infer that they were especially Italians, because I could only judge from their general appearance and complexion, and therefore I only meant to imply that they were of the type of the Latin races. In any case, I did not intend to cast any reflection on the Italian nation.
>
> This is the real truth, and therefore I feel honoured to give out the present statement.

The ambassador was evidently satisfied with this semi-vindication of his countrymen. He countersigned the statement, which was appended to the transcript.

Before leaving the United States Lowe paid a visit to Rene Harris. The widow had expressed a desire to testify, and had she done so, might have told of her encounters with the fifth officer on the *Carpathia* when she told him told him, 'Mr Lowe, you are wonderful. I want to thank you. I have no money, but when I get to New York I want to reward you.'

He had refused to accept the reward on the *Carpathia* and did so again when she tried to press it on him in New York. Lowe, who had a tendency to blush, reddened visibly. He replied, 'Mrs Harris, you make me blush. I have only done my duty. I won't take a penny for that. I only hollered. Anybody can holler.'[86]

CHAPTER 11

A BRITISH RECKONING

Most of the surviving officers and crew who had not already returned on the *Lapland* boarded the White Star liner *Adriatic* for the homeward voyage. Just before she sailed at midday on 2 May, Managing Director J. Bruce Ismay joined the ship, telling reporters he felt the US Inquiry thorough and that he bore no ill feeling towards the American public, despite being pilloried in their press.

Ismay went straight to his stateroom where he would remain for much of the voyage, just as he had done on the *Carpathia* immediately after the disaster when Clear Cameron claimed he 'ordered hot grog and a room for himself,' and 'never troubled himself to try and comfort the poor widows, the damn coward.'

Lowe's rebuke of the chairman earned her approval. 'Officer Lowe gave him socks before he left the *Titanic*,' she wrote in a letter. 'He didn't know who he was talking to and what's more he didn't care.'[87]

Lowe had even taken on the titled nobility on the *Carpathia*, if Rene Harris, writing twenty years after the event, is to be believed. She told of several shocked women huddled together in a secluded corner of the deck when they saw sailors hurrying by with lifebelts on. 'Good God! what's happened now?' cried one, voicing the fears of all, to which came the reply: 'Nothing, lady. Someone wants to take pictures.'[88]

The 'someone' was Sir Cosmo and Lady Duff Gordon, first-class passengers, who had survived in Boat 1 with just ten others. At this point, Rene Harris wrote, Harold Lowe intervened, and in no uncertain terms gave the Duff Gordons a dressing down. The photos were not taken – at least not then. The Duff Gordons got their souvenir snapshots in time, complete with lifebelts.

The homeward voyage was a calmer affair. Ismay at last ventured out, telling one passenger who engaged him in conversation that he felt American newspapers had judged him harshly without hearing his side of the story. Everyone also knew there would be more stories yet to be told; Lowe and his colleagues were far from free to resume their lives and careers on landfall. Back in England, the Board of Trade Inquiry into the disaster had begun on the day that the *Adriatic* sailed.

Lowe did not forget a promise to Sheriff Bayliss and when the *Adriatic* made her first port in home waters, at Queenstown, Ireland (*Titanic*'s last call), he sent a package to Sault Ste Marie, Michigan. It contained a tunic button from the uniform Lowe had worn the night the *Titanic* went down.

Bayliss was profoundly touched by the gesture, and wrote to Lowe, 'This token of remembrance is the most highly prized gift that I have ever received, and will be handed down to my son as a token of friendship given his Father by the man whom history will designate as the most heroic survivor of the *Titanic*.'

Bayliss' admiration for the man with whom he had had such a brief personal acquaintance was so strong that he had already framed a photo of Lowe from the *Illustrated London News* and took great pride in showing it to acquaintances who called on him as one of the heroes of the disaster that he had known personally. In writing to Lowe he noted that he would feel 'exceptionally honored' if the two were to remain in touch once Lowe's life had settled back into its routine.[89]

The *Adriatic* docked at the Liverpool Landing Stage at 7.30 a.m. on Saturday 11 May. A large group of relatives and press was kept waiting for three quarters of an hour before the passengers began to alight. Looking 'neat, dapper and well groomed,' Harold Lowe was among the first to emerge, to be greeted warmly by his father George. His sister Ada, now married to a Liverpool solicitor and living in the Wirral, was also there to meet him.

Any exhaustion Lowe exhibited in America had vanished with the week and a half he spent at sea as a simple passenger. He bore no apparent trace of his ordeal. The newspapers snapped photos and Lowe, who had been the focus of considerable interest in England following reports from America, 'attracted much attention from the crowd.' Stories concerning him had been circulating both from the America and from the *Titanic* crew that had already returned on the *Lapland*. Typical of these was the young second-class steward who arrived 'full of praise' for Lowe, declaring he had done as much as anyone to save lives.[90]

The newshounds were not to be disappointed. While other officers and crewmen managed to hold their tongues, Lowe soon modified his original comment to reporters that he had nothing to

tell them. With 'characteristic breeziness of diction' he first compli-
mented the British journalists on their manners.

Then Lowe went further. With 'a suggestive swing of the arm,' he
remarked of the American press that he would like to have 'some of
them shot on sight.'

It was proving very difficult for Lowe to suppress his habitual out-
spokenness, even though he had just been given a handwritten note
signed by J. Hemingway, deputy receiver of wreck, to 'Take notice that
you are hereby detained as a witness at the Board of Trade Inquiry
concerning the loss of the *Titanic*.' While some newspapers referred
only to Lowe being 'frank in his criticism of some of the newspapers
on the other side,' the *Liverpool Echo* ran his comments under the headline 'Interview With Mr Lowe – American Pressmen Denounced.'

The publicity must have taken on surreal dimensions for the
young officer, who had gone from anonymity to international
recognition in a few weeks. He arrived in England to find that his
testimony abroad had found a widespread audience, with even some
comment from surprising sources.

On 14 May, no less a figure than George Bernard Shaw launched
a scathing attack in *The Daily News* upon the idealisation of the
disaster by the public and press. The horror of the actual event had
been smothered in platitudes and hero worship, he argued, and he
particularly cited the romantic demand that 'officers must be calm,
proud, steady, [and] unmoved in the intervals of shooting the terrified foreigners.'

Turning to the Ismay incident, Shaw chastised, 'The actual evidence is that Mr Ismay was told by the officer of his boat to go to
hell, and that boats which were not full refused to go to the rescue
of those who were struggling in the water in cork jackets. Reason
frankly given: they were afraid. The fear was as natural as the officer's
language to Mr Ismay. Who of us dare blame them or feel sure that we
should have been any cooler or braver?' Yet the expectation was that
'everyone must face death without a tremor, and the band, according
to the *Birkenhead* precedent, must play *Nearer my God to Thee* as an
accompaniment to the invitation to Mr Ismay to go to hell.'

Shaw, understandably incensed at the gloss placed on stark tragedy,
demanded to know, 'What is the use of all this ghastly, blasphemous,
inhuman, braggartly lying?'

Arthur Conan Doyle, the author made famous by the creation of
Sherlock Holmes, responded with equal fervour to Shaw's opinion

piece, defending Harold Lowe from what he interpreted – inaccurately – as criticism of the *Titanic's* fifth officer.

'Mr Shaw's next suggestion – all the more poisonous because it is not put into so many words – is that the officers did not do their duty. If his vague words mean anything they can only mean this. He quotes as if it were a crime the words of Lowe to Mr Ismay when he interfered with his boat. I could not imagine a finer example of an officer doing his duty than that a subordinate should dare to speak thus to the managing director of the Line when he thought that he was impeding his life-saving work.'

As for the shooting of foreigners, Conan Doyle pressed on, 'The fact and assertion that these passengers were foreigners came from several eye witnesses. Does Mr Shaw think it should have been suppressed? If not what is he scolding about?'

As the literary lions grappled over heated words on the deck of a sinking ship, Lowe prepared to give his evidence in London. If the journalists hoped that Lowe's American utterances and first words back in Britain boded well for future copy, they were in for a disappointment. The Lowe that appeared at the Inquiry was an entirely more restrained man than the one who had 'quibbled and grown sarcastic' with Senator Smith.

On 22 May, he began his testimony:

'Harold Godfrey Lowe, is that your name?' He replied, 'Yes.'

He was then asked: 'Were you the Fifth Officer on the *Titanic*?' to which he responded: 'I had that honour.'

The flourish was uncharacteristic of his performance. For the most part he was to be monosyllabic in his responses, as if adhering to advice to say no more than absolutely necessary and to volunteer no information. There can be little doubt that such an attitude was at least partly imposed by the counsel for the White Star Line, but it is also likely that there was some latter day self-discipline coming into play as well.

The authority of the Board of Trade was recognised as wholly different to that of Senator Smith and his Senate Subcommittee. The Board had a power over the career of every mariner that the Americans did not remotely possess. Any or all of the *Titanic's* surviving officers could find themselves instantly deprived of their certificates and their livelihoods if the evidence was held to warrant it.

There was also something of a political minefield to be negotiated. 'A washing of dirty linen would help no one,' Lightoller later explained. 'The Board of Trade had passed that ship as in all respects fit for sea, in every sense of the word, with sufficient margin of safety for everyone on board. Now the Board of Trade was holding an inquiry into the loss of that ship – hence the whitewash brush.

'Personally I had no desire that blame should be attributed either to the Board of Trade or the White Star Line, although in all conscience it was a difficult task, when handled by some of the cleverest legal minds in England, striving tooth and nail to prove the inadequacy here, the lack there, when one had known, full well, and for many years, the ever-present possibility of just such a disaster.'

More formally structured than the American hearings, the physical environment of the British Inquiry was calculated to have a different psychological impact. Rather than sitting at a table as they had been with the senators in Washington, witnesses had to enter the dock at the cavernous Scottish Hall at Buckingham Gate.

At the second time of asking, Lowe treated the Ismay incident lightly. Asked what he had said to his managing director, Lowe allowed himself a chuckle as he replied, 'I think you know.' He got away with it – the galleries laughing with him – but it seems Lowe was reluctant to fuel interest in this particular episode. It likely would not bode well for his future career.

Other questions could not be avoided, including some that had not been pressed in Washington. Chief amongst these was how Lowe had come to leave the ship. He was examined on the point: 'Did you go by anybody's orders?' Lowe, who hadn't volunteered the information before, had evidently decided to be frank: 'I did not.'

He clarified: 'I saw five boats go away without an officer, and I told [Sixth Officer James] Moody on my own that I had seen five boats go away, and an officer ought to go in one of these boats. I asked him who it was to be – him or I – and he told me, 'You go; I will get in another boat.''

Lowe could have claimed that one of the dead officers had ordered him into a lifeboat and there would be no one to contradict. Although vulnerable to accusations that he had sought only to save his own life, Lowe's frankness on the point indicated that he stood by his actions. There was implied criticism in the follow-up question: 'I forget where [Moody] comes in order of seniority; is he senior to you or junior to you?'

Counsel suggestion was clear – that Lowe could have ordered Moody into the boat he himself had departed in. Lowe kept his answers short and chose not to elaborate on his last conversation with the sixth officer. But he had revised some of his US testimony – it was now five boats he had seen leave without an officer rather than three. It would make little sense for Lowe to deliberately exaggerate, as the Inquiry had access to the American testimony and sometimes quoted it back at witnesses in cases of inconsistency. Perhaps Lowe's recollection of details had instead become hazy. It was now five weeks since the ship had sunk.

There were some flashes of antagonism, either through indignation or defensiveness – similar to those he had shown in America when counsel for the third-class passengers cross-examined him on the question of returning with the lifeboat. But Lowe was keen to avoid appearing confrontational, as he had in America.

In answer to a question from Sir Robert Finlay about how many people were on Collapsible A when he rescued them, he responded, 'I don't know. I don't want to appear sarcastic, or anything like that, but you don't count people in a case like this. I should say, roughly, about twenty men and one woman.'

Lowe was recalled again the following day and questioned further about ice warnings and the chit he had seen in the chartroom, then released. The inquiry turned to technical matters, and men like naval architect Edward Wilding of Harland & Wolff took the stand to testify about the mechanics of the tragedy.

The question of the officers' certificates was touched on briefly, but confiscation was never seriously entertained. There was criticism, however, for both the deck officers and crew. Mersey's report had specific comments on the half-formed plan to load passengers into the lifeboats from the gangway doors, and suggested that the boats could have been held longer and filled with more passengers.

Mersey was careful to point out, 'I do not, however, desire these observations to be read as casting any reflection on the officers of the ship or on the crew who were working on the boat deck. They all worked admirably, but I think that if there had been better organisation the results would have been more satisfactory.'

The boats that had failed to return for survivors were remarked upon, particularly Boat 1, that of the Duff Gordons, that had held only twelve people, but Mersey concluded:

Subject to these few adverse comments, I have nothing but praise for both passengers and crew. All the witnesses speak well of their behaviour.

It is to be remembered that the night was dark, the noise of the escaping steam was terrifying, the peril, though perhaps not generally recognised, was imminent and great, and many passengers who were unable to speak or to understand English, were being collected together and hurried into the boats.

The evidence satisfies me that the officers did their work very well, and without any thought of themselves. Captain Smith, the Master, Mr Wilde, the Chief Officer, Mr Murdoch, the First Officer, and Mr Moody, the Sixth Officer, all went down with the ship while performing their duties. The others, with the exception of Mr Lightoller, took charge of boats and thus were saved.

Among the thousands avidly following the Inquiry, Lowe's evidence provided meagre comfort for the family of one of his deceased colleagues. His testimony about lifeboats 14 and 16 was printed in a Yorkshire newspaper by way of explanation as to why James Moody, the youngest and most junior officer, had not survived.

Moody's grieving family saved the article, placing it among the papers relating to their lost son, including the final bright and optimistic letters he had sent from Belfast and Southampton.

Although the surviving officers were photographed together for studio portraits in London, Lowe formed no close bond with his fellows. One of the remarks he made in later years about his colleagues served to doubt Lightoller's story of being blown free of the *Titanic* in a blast of air from the grating he was pinned against as the ship sank.

Lowe might not have had much faith in Lightoller's credibility, at least on this point, but there is little doubt that the older man had a warmth and charm coupled with professional ability that made him popular among other White Star Line colleagues. 'Lights' also seems to have had a genuine concern, and sense of responsibility, as the senior surviving deck officer, for both the survivors and the families of the dead.

Lowe's aloofness, on the other hand, may have extended to White Star circles in general. Brian Mainwaring, a retired White Star officer, wrote in 1956 of his familiarity with Lightoller ('a charming fellow

and very able officer') as well as Pitman and Boxhall, but mused that
he had often wondered what became of Lowe.

It is curious that Lowe should be left out; his subsequent career
followed closely that of Boxhall, and yet it would seem he wasn't
prominent in the officer gossip. Lowe never did display much apti-
tude for the 'greasy pole' of company advancement. And he was
always more likely to return to the family home in Wales between
voyages than to spend time in port with his colleagues.

There is some suggestion that Harold Lowe left the Inquiry in
London for the last time on 24 May 1912. After a few days' holiday,
possibly in Colwyn Bay, on the afternoon of 29 May he arrived
home at last in Barmouth.

The people there had expressed considerable enthusiasm at
the exploits of their home-grown hero. The *Barmouth & County
Advertiser and District Weekly News* reported on 25 April the 'heroism
which was evidently displayed by [Officer Lowe] under the most
trying circumstances imaginable.' It was also disclosed that moves
were afoot by his 'old friends and comrades' to acknowledge this
son of Barmouth. Flyers were distributed with a photo of Harold in
Elder Dempster uniform, headlined: 'An Appreciation of Heroism.'
The committee's purpose was set out: 'The many friends, acquaintances, and admirers of the gallant young Officer – MR HAROLD
G LOWE – who distinguished himself so conspicuously in connection with the sad disaster of the *Titanic*, are anxious to give some
practical expression of their appreciation of his heroic conduct.'

The response to the call for recognition was enthusiastic. The
form of presentation was to be determined by the amount collected, and by the closing date of 18 May a substantial sum had
amassed. John Walters, owner of the local 'picture palace' offered the
use of his Pavilion for the ceremony, and a date was set for Friday
21 June 1912.

It was standing room only at the ceremony. Lowe's sweetheart,
Nellie, was amazed at the number of people who swarmed over
the roof trusses and other vantage points. The local population had
determined that Harold Lowe would 'prove an exception to the idea
that a prophet is not honoured in his own country,' as the *Advertiser*
put it. Lowe himself looked every bit the part, obliging a request of
the organisers that he wear his White Star uniform.

The evening began with a short film presentation, as Mr Walters
displayed newsreel footage of images connected to the recent

disaster. The first projection on screen was Harold Lowe himself, which met with enthusiastic cheering. A montage of *Titanic* clips followed – including the launch, leaving Southampton, icebergs in the sea lanes, the arrival of the SS *Carpathia* with survivors in New York, the departure of the *Mackay-Bennett* to pick up bodies, and the funeral of bandmaster Wallace Hartley at Colne.

As the images flickered over the screen, soft music filtered through the room, provided by the Barmouth Silver Coronation Band hidden behind the stage scenery. Their melody was 'Nearer My God to Thee'. The vast audience fell to silence as scenes of the funeral were shown, but by the time Mr Jones of the committee took to the stage to begin the presentation, was back to 'a high pitch of enthusiasm.'

Jones began:

> When the sad news of the loss of the *Titanic* reached this town, and when it was known that one of Barmouth's young men was an officer on board, the anxiety for his safety was intense.
>
> A day or two later, however, the reports showed that not only was he saved himself, but that he had, by his gallant conduct, been the means of saving a large number of other lives. His friends and admirers thought that they would like to do something practical to prove their appreciation of his devotion to his duty.
>
> No sooner was the matter mooted than money in small sums of thruppence and upwards poured in with the result that tonight a valuable token of the esteem in which the young officer is held, will be presented to him.'

Mr Jones called upon the Revd Gwynore Davies, chairman of the committee, to make the presentation. The latter enthused: 'A more inspiring sight than that which is before me now I have seldom if ever seen. It is a sight anyone might be proud of. Here we find this huge pavilion thronged with people representing all classes in the town and district brought together to do honour to our brave young fellow townsman.' He continued:

> I am not sure which feeling is the stronger in my heart and yours this evening – whether it is the feeling of sadness when we think of the awful calamity connected with the *Titanic* or joy that so many were saved. Of one thing I am certain, and that is that our hearts go up in thankfulness to Almighty God that in his goodness he was

pleased to use a young man from Barmouth as an instrument in His hands to save so many of our fellow men.

He turned to Lowe:

> Now my young friend I consider it a privilege to hand you this gold watch and chain as a token of the admiration felt towards you by a large circle of friends in and around Barmouth. We are proud of you; and whenever you look upon this watch and feel its ticking, remember that there are warm hearts thinking of you. Your heroic conduct is the admiration of the people of two Continents.
>
> God bless you and may you rise higher and higher as you sail over the deep is our earnest prayer.

When the cheering subsided somewhat, he continued:

> In addition to the gold watch and chain I have much pleasure, on behalf of Mrs Henry B. Harris, New York, to present you with this fine set of Marine instruments, which I understand are very valuable and the best money could procure.
>
> When acting as you did on the fearful night you had no thought of any reward, but did your duty nobly from the goodness of your heart, yet it is a satisfaction to you that your brave and heroic conduct is appreciated on both sides of the Atlantic.

The remarks were greeted by more loud ovations.

Now the Revd Davies broached a more cumbersome subject. 'I don't know whether you have yet fixed on a partner for life or not…' he paused for effect as Harold and Nellie wondered what was to follow and elements of the crowd grew ribald. 'Remember this is a leap year and I have a shrewd notion that you have already received a number of proposals. It may not be long before we shall meet in this pavilion to welcome you home with an American millionairess!'

The venture was met with 'great cheering,' although what Nellie thought of it is not recorded. She may even have been grateful for a clerical nudge in the officer's ribs.

The presentation watch, worth the princely sum of £36 10s, was inscribed on the reverse with Lowe's monogram. Inside were the words: 'Presented to Harold G. Lowe, 5th Officer RMS *Titanic*, by friends of his in Barmouth and elsewhere, in recognition and appreciation of his gallant services at the foundering of the *Titanic*, 15th April 1912.' Accompanying this was an 'Album of names of subscribers'.

The nautical instruments, consisting of a sextant, naval telescope and high-powered binoculars were each inscribed 'To Harold Godfrey Lowe, 5th Officer RMS *Titanic*. "The real hero of the *Titanic*." With deepest gratitude from Mrs Henry B. Harris of New York.'

Lowe, who had given a smart naval salute when ascending the stage to receive his gifts, modestly thanked the audience for the kind manner in which they received him. He diligently reeled off a list of names of committee members who had gone to so much trouble in organising the event. But when it came to speaking of the disaster, it all became too overwhelming for him and his distress was evident to those in the hall.

The *Barmouth Advertiser*, in publishing its account, decided that a few verses would be appropriate to the occasion:

To Harold G Lowe

Pattern to your sex and country
Noble-hearted, kind and brave,
Willing to assist the needy,
In distress, alert to save.

From the jaws of death God saved thee,
Answered all our anxious prayers.
May He from care and danger
Keep thee free in future years.

So wear thou, now, this crown of love.
Neat-woven for they brow
By hearts that beat with gratitude
And love thee truly now.

Lowe would be presented with more small remembrances. From the Barmouth Intermediate School, his alma mater, came a gold matchbox. From the other side of the world, Mary and Sara Compton sent him a match case inscribed 'In Gratitude'. To the chain of his new gold watch he affixed the sovereign presented to him by a male survivor on the *Carpathia*.

More mundane souvenirs survive today. Scrawled in the back of Lowe's notebook are percentage breakdowns of the survivors from each class. They sit side by side with a few calculations Lowe made regarding his expense claims for appearances at the inquiries.

But the reckoning, however much an attempt at discipline, was not without remorse. Even as a rescuer, Lowe was a candidate for survivors' guilt. It would have become apparent to him as soon as Boat 14 first began to pull through the wreckage and bodies that his delay had proved fatal for most of those he wished to save. It was a point hammered home at both inquiries through close questioning on why he had waited so long.

Although he emphatically insisted that he had to wait as long as he did, his replies struck an occasionally defensive note. As early as July 1912, Lowe alluded to his regrets when accepting the gold match box from his old school. He was glad that he had been able to save some lives, he said, but regretted he had not saved more.

More than the standard rhetoric of modesty, the pain may have deepened with the years. The *Titanic* would always be a subject that he actively avoided discussing. For the reminder of his life, even hearing the psalm 'Nearer My God To Thee' evoked a profound emotion in Lowe, now that it was inescapably entangled with memories of that terrible night.

There are indications that he went to earth that summer following the disaster. Sixth Officer Moody's father, desperate for news, had written to him. Lowe, who answered other letters personally, asked his father to respond to this one. Perhaps this death in particular was still difficult for Lowe to deal with.

Yet he began a scrapbook on the tragedy, collating all the material he had assembled since the *Carpathia* arrived in New York. Whatever he thought of the American press, he carefully kept the newspapers. He put clippings from them into a *Titanic* album, alongside postcards of the ship he had bought in Belfast. One of these showed the *Titanic* (looking more like the *Olympic*) steaming past the Statue of Liberty. James Moody had sent one to his sister on 1 April – April Fool's Day – saying, 'This is, of course, rather a faked photo as this ship has never been through the water & the background shows New York, but it's a very good likeness.'[91]

The articles he kept included coverage of his own testimony and that of others about him, miscellaneous survivor accounts, and many articles naming Rene Harris. Commemorative sheet music, memorial leaflets, photos of the ship, a photograph of his arrival in Liverpool – all these he kept, and one of his most carefully worked sketches is a depiction of the *Titanic*.

Eventually it was time for Lowe to pick up the threads of his career. Lowe went back to Liverpool and filled out an application for a copy of his Master's certificate. In the space to record 'place, date, occasion, and cause of the loss of the certificate', he noted 'on board the *Titanic* in the mid Atlantic on the 15th April, 1912'. The usual fee for a replacement was waived.

CHAPTER 12

IN PEACE AND WAR

When Lowe went back to sea it was not to the North Atlantic run; his brief stint on the Western Ocean was over. Instead it was back to the long Australian voyages, and that August he was assigned to the *Medic*. Like many of his *Titanic* colleagues he turned to the only profession he knew. Some of the shipwrecked stokers, stewards and deckhands, under financial pressure, had resumed working on liners as soon as they had returned to England or were released from testimony.

Lizelle Simpson, sister of the *Titanic*'s lost Assistant Surgeon John Simpson, was also travelling aboard the *Medic*, visiting her sister in Melbourne. The Simpson family had already been in contact with Second Officer Lightoller, who remembered exchanging a joke with the young doctor very shortly before the ship's final plunge. Now Lizelle sought out the *Medic*'s third officer to see if he could provide any more information on her brother's final hours. Lowe, who had made Dr Simpson's acquaintance on the *Titanic*, was able to tell her that Simpson had rendered him assistance during the loading of the lifeboats by fetching an electric torch. Grateful for this piece of news, slight though it was, Lizelle told Lowe that the family would be very happy to receive him in their home in Belfast should he ever happen to return to the north of Ireland.

A little bad luck now befell Harold Lowe. According to Simpson's correspondence, he suffered a broken leg in October 1912 on the *Medic*'s outward voyage. The injury was a severe one and necessitated Lowe's confinement to bed, where he had ample time to ponder the irony of having emerged unscathed from catastrophe only to find himself injured on his next vessel. Curiously, the *Medic*'s official log contains no reference to the incident, although by law it should have been recorded.

The *Medic* arrived in Cape Town on 24 August after a passage of three weeks. Her call was brief, and that evening she was underway again to arrive just over a fortnight later in Melbourne, where the

Medic remained for five days. Simpson took her uncle and cousin to the ship's infirmary to introduce them to Lowe.

'Flora and I took some fruit & flowers and went to see him this afternoon again,' wrote Lizelle. 'It is very dull for him as he is not allowed to get up at all.' Lowe had two months to recuperate on the return voyage as the *Medic* called at Port Natal, Cape Town and Plymouth. She arrived back in Liverpool on 1 December.[92]

His voyage to Australia had not gone unnoticed. The Australian edition of *Punch* ran a small piece on the *Medic*'s officer the week after she left Melbourne, noting that an opportunity had been missed by the 'lion-hunting, hero-worshipping public' who had been unaware of the identity of the ship's third officer. 'A great fuss has been made of him in the English and American papers,' it ran. 'He is a young man, and it is supposed that he has been sent out on the Australian-Cape trade, so that he may be free from lionising for a time.'

Lowe was not the only lionised figure on board his next vessel, the *Gothic*, again on the Australia run. Champion sculler Henry 'Harry' Pearce joined the ship in Sydney, the first step in his journey to challenge world champion sculler Ernest Barry that July on the Thames. Henry 'Footy' Pearce (so nicknamed for his large feet, but whom Harold called 'Harry') had evolved his skills while working as a dory boatman in Sydney harbour, picking up cargo from ships unable to berth at the wharfs. Harry's competitive edge led him to stage races against other boats, and the turn of speed he developed in loading, reaching shore, unloading and returning to the ships meant a higher turnover for his business. Perhaps it was their shared experience in small boats that lead the two to develop a friendship that was to remain steadfast over many years. Lowe and Pearce were photographed together aboard the *Gothic* and again in London and the photographs in his album indicate that Lowe was on hand to see Pearce's unsuccessful bid to defeat Barry at Henley. Before sailing, Pearce had complained of those in Australia who had harassed him to row challengers while he was focused on preparing for his race against the world champion. He did make a point of telling reporters that the White Star officials had treated him well, and made arrangements for him to train on board.[93]

Lowe continued to receive messages of appreciation for his role in the *Titanic* disaster well into the next year, as he indicated to Selena Cook in a letter of March 1913. Cook had been one of the passengers of Boat 14 who spoke to the newspapers about her admiration for Lowe and her letter was waiting for him in Durban on the return leg of this second voyage to Australia on the *Gothic*. Thanking her for the letter, which had followed him 'all round the world,' he commented, 'Several survivors of the *Titanic* have written letters to me, but I fancy they have been rather too glowing, any way I suppose it is from their hearts. Although I did not do much on that awful night, my only hope is that I, or any other person that went through it, will not witness or go through another similar experience again.' He assured her that he was trying to move on, adding, 'I have not quite been standing still.'[94]

In mid-1913 the White Star Line informed Lowe that he had been called up for a month's training in the Royal Naval Reserve. RNR records are incomplete, but it appears that he trained aboard HMS *Hogue* at Chatham Naval Station, travelling 30 miles by train from London to catch a picket boat out to the vessel, one of dozens of warships moored in the harbour.

Merchant officers training for the first time had to accustom themselves to the ancient and sometimes rigid traditions of the Royal Navy. Lowe was soon found to be a fit and proper person to hold a commission in the RNR, and his sub-lieutenant's commission was confirmed on 14 June 1913.

Events were also moving forward in his personal life, as no doubt the Revd Davies was delighted to hear. Lowe's long courtship with Nellie finally ended on 24 September when they married at St Paul's church in Colwyn Bay. Circumstances dictated that the newlyweds should move in with Nellie's father, William, at Bryn Mostyn. William Whitehouse was in poor health and required constant nursing care. Lowe's long absences at sea in any case militated against the couple setting up on their own. At least the Colwyn Bay address was conveniently located for travel to the Liverpool docks.

World events were moving quickly too. Lowe's active involvement in the Royal Navy Reserve and his interest in politics would have made him well aware of what was ahead, had not the coming cataclysm long thrown its shadow before it. Nowhere had the building hostility between Britain and Germany been more apparent than in the race for sea supremacy, both in merchant and naval fleets.

In April 1914, Lowe was called up for twelve months' training on warships to qualify as a lieutenant. His first appointment was to HMS *Excellent*, at the naval gunnery school in Portsmouth. In June he was officially reassigned to the HMS *Victory* barracks. His training coincided with a growing clamour of nationalism and diplomatic posturing that seemed to hasten the inevitable armed hostilities. In the middle of it came news that Nellie was pregnant with their first child. Lowe may not have had the chance to hurry home. Later that summer, on 29 July 1914, the Admiralty sent a 'Warning Telegram' to the fleets, followed by an order from the government for full naval mobilisation on 1 August.

The next day – two days before Great Britain declared war on Germany – Lowe sat down and made out his will.

August 2nd '14

I leave everything to my wife & anything I may inherit.

H. G. Lowe
Lieut. RNR

As it turned out, the outbreak of war meant no immediate change, and he remained essentially a landlubber. If he was keen to see action, there was at least some compensation, because on 20 November – the eve of his own birthday – Harold and Nellie's daughter, Florence Josephine Edge, was born. It seems Harold was at last able to obtain leave from his training, as he reported the birth to the registry office.

Although not yet actively serving, 1915 saw Lowe qualify as a lieutenant, obtaining the rank that July. Then came more good news for the Lowe family, as Nellie was able to tell her husband she was pregnant again.

On 2 January 1916, Harold Lowe was officially assigned to active service and despatched to the cruiser HMS *Donegal*. The *Donegal*, launched in September 1902, was of some 9,800 tons and 463½ft in length. She was armed with .45 calibre guns, anti-aircraft and machine guns, and was equipped with torpedo tubes and armour plating. Lieutenant Lowe joined her at Scapa Flow. For the next few weeks she would do little but patrol local waters. A month and a half later, on 20 February, the *Donegal* departed for Liverpool and a refit, entering dry dock. Lowe's frustration as a self-avowed man of action can best be imagined.

For the next fortnight her crew patiently waited for her to be allowed put to sea again, but when she did, on 5 March, she didn't get far. One of her tugs fouled the *Donegal*'s port propeller. She put back into berth, and that evening divers examined the propeller. The following day she was back in the graving dock, but the setback proved temporary and by 8 March she set course for the return to Scapa Flow.

This was the monotony of war for many of the men aboard the cruisers. They spent long stints in Scapa, followed by intervals of patrolling the coast on the lookout for mines, mystical U-boats, and elusive commerce raiders. The *Donegal*'s log records protracted periods when the only activity was routine ship's business.

Nellie was now approaching full term with her second pregnancy, but there was no question of Harold obtaining leave. He could only anxiously await news from home indicating the welfare of mother and child, word that finally arrived on 21 March, when he learned he had a son and heir. The boy would bear the names of his father and both grandfathers, Harold William George. Nellie reported the birth to the registry office the month after young Harold was born. Lowe, when he finally had the chance to meet his newborn son, was overwhelmed with tenderness and pride. Nellie woke one night to find her husband standing by the baby's crib, holding his child in his arms and looking at him with wonder. But this was war and soon he was away again with HMS *Donegal*, attached to the 7th Cruiser Squadron of the Grand Fleet and involved in the hunt for the legendary German raider *Möewe*. It was a chase without success.

The Germans did not inflict damage on the *Donegal,* but the sea herself posed a potentially lethal threat. On 26 March 1916, the vessel was struck by an enormous wave, and the Bosun and nine ratings were injured. She returned to Scapa yet again.

Elsewhere the war was inflicting heavy damage on men and material. Many of Lowe's old ships, particularly the Elder Dempster vessels, fell victim to U-boat attacks. One such, the *Addah*, on which he had served for over a year, was sent to the bottom on 15 June 1917. She was travelling from Montreal to Cherbourg with general cargo when UC-69 struck with a single torpedo. Captain Clarke ordered his crew to abandon ship, but then had his gunner open fire with the stern gun, hitting the U-boat yet failing to seriously damage her. Clarke and the gunner jumped overboard and were picked up by one of the lifeboats, but the angered U-boat promptly rammed the frail craft and sank her. UC-69 then fired upon the survivors, killing eight.

On 31 May 1916 came the large-scale naval engagement many
had predicted since the war began, but the *Donegal* was to narrowly
miss out on the Battle of Jutland. Shortly before, she was sent on
detached service and assigned to duties that took her out of home
waters. Christmas 1916 was spent in Sierra Leone, well away from
home.

While there were no combat casualties, there were other mishaps
aboard. In January 1917, Stoker Adam Boyd was smothered by a slide
of coal in one of the ship's bunkers. The death was logged at 1.30 p.m.,
and he was buried at sea five hours later. Some tradition was observed
amid the haste – that being the time-honoured Royal Navy ritual of
auctioning off his belongings to raise money for his family.

On 24 February the *Donegal* arrived in Bermuda, very distant
from the mud in Flanders, but it was here that Lowe learned of a
transfer, and on 30 March he was discharged. He disembarked from
the *Donegal* and boarded a supply ship to return to England. En
route he received orders assigning him again to HMS *Excellent*, the
Portsmouth gunnery training base.

There was time for a brief family reunion. An image has survived
from this short interval before he was sent away to war again, encap-
sulating the joys of homecoming. Lowe wears his RNR uniform
with Josie beside him and young Harold, barely more than a baby,
on his knee. Dark-eyed Josie has a hand clamped possessively on the
knee of a parent who was almost a stranger.

By June 1917 Lieutenant Lowe was aboard HMS *Suffolk*, departing Plymouth for Sierra Leone en route to South Africa and the
Far East, escorting the SS *Balmoral Castle*. As they went southwards
and the weather warmed, the officers on the *Suffolk* donned their
summer whites. They passed through the latitudes of the flying fish,
a fact announced when one landed aboard only to be swiftly com-
mandeered by the Master-at-Arms Herbert Simpkins for breakfast.
She arrived in Sierra Leone on 13 June, where several ratings were
discharged to detention quarters. The warm weather gave two crewmen sunstroke severe enough to require hospitalisation.

On 23 June, as they crossed the line, the *Balmoral Castle* was
brought up on the *Suffolk*'s starboard side to give her passengers a
good view of Neptune's Court which had been assembled on the
decks of the cruiser for the traditional Crossing the Line ceremony.
Accompanied by the *Suffolk*'s band playing on the bridge, the
captain and the officers paraded on the well deck. Then Neptune

himself, played by W. Greens, gave a speech, and then presented the captain with 'Order of the Flying Fish' medals. The camera-keen on the *Suffolk* snapped photos before the captain and the court marched around to the upper deck where mock battles were staged, thoroughly enjoyed by the participating ratings. It was a more elaborate court than the first such Crossing the Line ceremonies in which Lowe had participated during his earliest days in sail. In addition to Neptune himself and the obligatory 'Queen Amphitrite', a sailor in drag, there was a secretary, chaplain, doctor, barber, and dozens of assorted 'policemen' and 'seabears'.

Continuing southward the weather once again turned cold as they entered the Southern Hemisphere's winter, and by the end of June they were in their winter uniforms as they approached South Africa. They arrived off Cape Town on the morning of 4 July and parted ways with the *Balmoral Castle*, the liner entering the harbour and the cruiser going on to Simonstown, arriving there on a misty and chilly afternoon. From Cape Town they went on to Durban, a city at least one of the *Suffolk*'s crew thought very fine, 'clean and healthy, lovely buildings and very wide streets, and lovely surroundings. Parks Botanical Gardens, Zoo, etc. fine harbour and sea front.'[95]

Leaving Durban they hit heavy weather, as the southern oceans lived up to their reputation. The *Suffolk* ran straight into strong winds and rough seas over the side, and as night came on the wind only increased and the seas rose. The men battened her down as the mess decks flooded and the ship rolled heavily. Even when the men were able to work about the upper deck a few seas came inboard and it was necessary to keep the hatchways closed. It was to continue like this for almost a week, and at one point she had to ease down head to the wind for twelve hours. Eventually, however, it cleared and the stars became visible once again.

Word of the progress of the war in Europe reached the ship's crew by wireless, and they heard with astonishment of air raids on Essex and then on London itself, events that made a marked impression on the men and indicated the shape of more terrible war to come. The wireless also conveyed instructions from HQ, and on 17 September the *Suffolk* was ordered to Penang for convoy escort duties.

Not all the ships in the convoy were entirely seaworthy and on 25 September disaster struck. The transport vessel *Merban*, already wallowing in heavy seas, began to rapidly make water, and within an hour had foundered. All her crew managed to get off safely, except for the captain, who opted to go down with his ship. The *Suffolk* lowered boats to pull around where she had gone down in an attempt to recover his body, but the sea did not give him up. With the escapees on board, they proceeded with the other three ships in the convoy.

On 28 September, *Suffolk* rendezvoused with HMS *Venus* and handed over the convoy to the latter's care. Yet the following day brought a fresh distress message – the *Venus* wiring for assistance after she and another transport had run afoul of monsoon conditions. There was no immediate danger but the *Suffolk* returned at her best possible speed of 17 knots, locating the struggling convoy on 1 October. The *Venus* had a hawser fouling one of her propellers and was steaming with only one engine, making slow progress. As she laboured on her way, the *Suffolk* took the lame convoy ship in tow, using oil night and day to keep down the seas. They made Colombo two days later.

There was good war news from the European front waiting for her there, and the crew were able to unwind with a game of rugby against a local team. Overall, however, the town was very quiet, with most lights out early and shipping in the port scarce. They sailed again on 8 October, passing HMS *Venus* still making her slow way to Colombo towing one of the convoy ships.

A few days later a smallpox case was discovered among the survivors of the *Merban* still on board. They increased their speed as they made for Penang and vaccinated all men who hadn't already been inoculated. Arriving at the Malaysian port they discharged the survivors and received a welcome delivery of mail.

In mid-December, while at Plover Cover, the *Suffolk* received orders to proceed at all possible speed to Harrison's Straits in the South China Sea, about 250 miles distant, in order to attempt the rescue of a French steamer that was badly stranded. No sooner had she got underway than a Chinese junk crossed her bow and only narrowly managed to avoid the full force of the *Suffolk*'s ram. The smaller vessel caught the cruiser on the starboard quarter and carried away handrails on the aft shelter deck – what damage the junk suffered was not recorded, being considered a matter of rather less importance than damage to one of His Majesty's ships. Proceeding slowly in the hazy weather and shallow waters they tried to get close to the stranded steamer but the French vessel was tantalisingly out of reach as the weather was too bad to venture closer. Reluctantly they had to turn away, reporting as much to headquarters and leaving the rescue to others to accomplish.

Lowe's scrapbooks of his time aboard the *Suffolk*, carefully compiled, hint at the stories and experiences that have no place in the log of a warship. Photos of the lieutenant in his whites, complete with a pith helmet, both riding and driving camels in the style of a charioteer, suggest adventures in foreign ports and the camaraderie of the off-duty hours on shore leave. Aden and the Suez Canal, Malta, Shanghai, Hong Kong, Singapore, Minikoi Island – patrolling the interests of her nation and her allies in the days when the British Empire still spanned the world give this record of the *Suffolk*'s journey something of the aspect of an exotic travelogue. When ashore, they played local sporting teams or attended concerts 'got up' for their amusement by the local ex-patriot community. In between shore leaves the men had to be kept occupied with drill and the eternal round of maintenance, from washing and mending their own personal items to the constant chipping and painting of the ship herself.

Christmas came and the *Suffolk* lay in Hong Kong harbour. It was a quiet day on board, although some of the men went ashore in the evening to take their dinner in a more festive atmosphere. In the following days the rumours grew that they were to put to sea again. Confirmation came on 4 January 1918, when officials came on board to oversee new heating arrangements. The next day was occupied with fixing steam pipes and stoves, and the bringing aboard of stores and winter clothing. They might have joked that they must be heading for Siberia. As it turned out, they were.

CHAPTER 13

THE BOLSHEVIK BUSINESS

As she lay at Hong Kong, the *Suffolk* received orders that were to involve her in one of the great upheavals of the twentieth century. She was to proceed to Vladivostok where, as Lowe's son phrased it in later years, Bolshevik revolutionaries were being something of a 'nuisance'. British, American, Japanese, Canadian and French forces would all eventually be involved in the ensuing civil war. Since the collapse of the Tsarist regime in 1917 the new Soviet government had aimed at an armistice with Germany. The Allies, alarmed at the prospect of the Kaiser thereby being able to divert resources to the Western Front, began to contemplate direct action. It hardened to firm resolve when in December 1917 the Treaty of Brest-Litovsk brought the First World War to an end on the Eastern Front.

A little-recognised ally now came to the fore. Japan was already engaged in the worldwide conflagration but her large, well-trained military had been limited thus far to small actions against German colonies in the Pacific. The Russian anti-Bolshevik groups coalesced under the leadership of Admiral Kolchak, who formed a government at Omsk that covered geographic territory over half of Russia, from Lake Baikal almost to the Volga. Kolchak was recognised by the Allies and from the beginning of 1919 war supplies had been dispatched to the White Russians, up to and including British service uniforms. The attack upon the Soviets was multi-pronged, with Deniken in the south, Franco-Ukrainian forces in the Ukraine, General Yudenich in the north-west (with British naval support) preparing to advance on Petrograd and Kolchak himself directing most of his forces to link with the Whites around Archangel. While the French proposed multilateral intervention against Russia, the Japanese now proposed acting alone against Siberia. As the strategists dithered, Britain in time-honoured tradition sent a gunboat – Harold Lowe's.

After calling at Japan and entertaining a visiting Admiral in command of Japanese operations that had already begun on Russia's

Pacific coast, the *Suffolk* sailed for Vladivostok. The temperature
was now dropping noticeably, with snowstorms sharpening the icy
atmosphere. When the vessel arrived in January 1918, it was only
after steaming through dense ice fields. Harold Lowe now had
unwanted experience of ice in three different oceans and land was
a decidedly welcome sight. They arrived to find Japanese battleships
in the harbour, many of them frozen in. At least one man was prepared to give them a warm welcome – the British consul, no doubt
relieved at this tangible evidence of his country's interest. He came
on board and conferred with Captain Payne.

The next morning found all ships icebound. It was only after ice-
breakers did their work that the *Suffolk* was able to move closer to
shore, where she anchored. The cruiser *Iwami* had arrived just prior to
the *Suffolk*, and a few days later Tokyo despatched another, the *Ashani*,
which arrived just after her Royal Navy ally. The British crew mar-
velled at the furry spectacle the Japanese cruiser made as she steamed
into the port, robed in snow and ice. Lowe photographed her.

Although things were quiet when they arrived, the briefing to
Captain Payne was that 'things in general are in a very bad state.'
Ostensibly the *Suffolk* was there to protect the port's 648,000 tons
of stores and sundry British nationals in what was an increasingly
volatile situation. Soon the USS *Brooklyn* was despatched there from
Yokohama, in part as a reminder to the Japanese that America had
her own interests in the region.

Vladivostok had emerged as Russia's primary port and naval base
in the east following the completion of the Trans-Siberian Railway
and the loss of Port Arthur in the Russian-Japanese war. With the
advent of the First World War it became the entry point for arms
and materiel from North America aimed at bolstering Russia's war
effort. While the presence of Allied cruisers ensured that Vladivostok
was the only large Siberian city not yet under Bolshevik control by
early 1918, Marxist forces were nonetheless at work in the town.

It was hard to keep up morale in the face of extreme weather and
a keen sense of isolation. Nor had the *Suffolk* done anything except
to maintain a 'presence', making her little more than a floating pawn
in a very large game. February dragged into March, blizzards and a
kind of bleary bleakness alternated with one another, and Captain
Payne was obliged to warn the men of the dangers of drink ashore.

The men of the *Suffolk* and *Brooklyn* were now being targeted
by the Bolshevik sympathisers and propagandists within the town,

where there was already a vigorous revolutionary press that was powered in the main by a single man, Editor Jerome A. Lifschitz. Of particular offence to Lifschitz was the presence of the Allied warships which stood between the Bolsheviks and undisputed control of Vladivostok. 'You have ordered your warships to come and stay in our harbour, under the pretext of protecting your precious lives and property,' he wrote. 'But you are really here to threaten and bully us in our work of social and economic reconstruction.'

'In emancipating ourselves from the yoke of slavery we shall not stand alone! We shall be joined by the workers of the world in that holy fight of freeing ourselves from the shirkers of the world! You may see the handwriting on the wall...'[96]

The sailors and marines of the *Suffolk* and *Brooklyn* did not see any such hand and were reluctant to throw off their oppressor officers as urged to do. Meanwhile those officers who went ashore inevitably came into contact with the tensions of the city. Lifschitz wrote of his being stopped near the docks by a petty officer of the *Suffolk* who told him that whatever happened he would be the first to be shot 'accidentally'.

The generalised mood in the powder-keg port inevitably exploded into violence. On 4 April, a group of men in Bolshevik uniforms demanded money at gunpoint from a Japanese shopkeeper. When he refused, he and two other Japanese were shot dead. It provided Tokyo with precisely the justification for action that they had sought, and by the next morning 500 marines had gone ashore for the protection of Japanese lives and property. Captain Payne also took action, the *Suffolk* despatching fifty marines to form a cordon around the British consulate.

The Americans opted not to make a similar move, a course of action that proved prudent as the Bolsheviks now used the Japanese and British 'aggression' to whip up public hostility. It proved so deadly that the marines of both nations were soon hastily withdrawn. For weeks the situation teetered on the precipice. On 25 April, as one of the Allied transports sailed for San Francisco, news arrived of a massacre of Russians ashore. A party of marines was landed to investigate, and returned to report that the Bolsheviks had torched nearly two dozen houses and killed twenty-nine.

A few days later the *Suffolk* sent ashore her musicians and some of her men to attend the funeral of the victims, with American and Russian bands also attending. Just before the funeral cortege passed

off, some Bolsheviks swept past in a carriage and hurled a bomb
into the procession. It missed its mark. Fire was returned, killing one
bomber as well as a horse and driver.

The Bolsheviks were becoming increasingly confident and
the renewed withdrawal of British and Japanese marines per-
suaded them that they could act. On 2 May, large forces of armed
Bolsheviks moved into the city from the countryside without opposition. Vladivostok was Red.

But there was to be one more twist in the tale.

It is one of history's quirks that a legion of Czech troops was
converging on the region. The soldiers had originally formed a
reluctant component of the Austrian-Hungarian army in the west.
Most had then taken the first opportunity to surrender willingly to
the Russians, and about 40,000 were then formed into several regiments to fight on the side of the Allies.

With the collapse of Tsarist Russia they became prisoners of
circumstance that the Soviets were now anxious to have off their
soil. The Czech National Council negotiated their evacuation
with the Bolsheviks and it was agreed to allow them to escape via
Vladivostok. The Czechs now began their rail journey to what had
been an open city, only to see it close just before they got there.
The Bolshevik seizure now proved to be a significant miscalcula-
tion. Thwarted in their attempt to reach the Pacific, and suddenly
alarmed by a directive from Trotsky ordering that they be disarmed
and formed into labour battalions, the Czechs now took matters
into their own hands. Fighting broke out along a line of railway
towns as the Czechs launched their savagely glorious bid to reach
the sea. In many instances they had the advantage over the Red
Army in both numbers and discipline, and soon succeeded in con-
trolling large sections of the Trans-Siberian line and many of the
larger towns.

The original regiments had also been strengthened by Czechs
and Slovaks exiled in Russia before the war only to be recruited
into service on the eastern front. By July 1918 the numbers of the
Czech Legion had increased to over 70,000. As they poured into
Vladivostok, they ripped apart the Bolshevik organisation. The
Czechs were coming.

On 28 June, the sergeant-at-arms of the *Suffolk* made a matter-of-
fact entry in his diary: 'Fine weather. Arrangements made to disarm
the Bolsheviks on Saturday. All seamen told off for landing.' In sup-

porting the Czechs, the Allies suddenly had both a rallying point and a formidable military force that might ultimately be redeployed to the Western Front.

Such are the vagaries of war, and on the misty morning of Saturday 29 June, at 8.30 a.m., a Czech ultimatum was delivered to Soviet commissar Konstantin Sukhanov, calling for an unconditional surrender of his men, the evacuation of offices, and for Red soldiers to proceed to the high school field to be disarmed. A 30-minute deadline was given. When Sukhanov rushed to the Czech head-quarters and asked permission to call Moscow, he was summarily placed under arrest.

A visiting Congregationist minister, the Revd Albert Rhys Williams, came across a Soviet commissar having his shoes blacked near the Red Fleet building. The commissar explained: 'In a few minutes I may be dangling from a lamppost, and I want to be as nice looking a corpse as possible.'[97]

Czech troops filled the streets, landing in boats from across the bay, while the Allied ships sent in their own men in support. At 10.10 a.m. the *Suffolk* landed small arms companies and maxim gun crews, Officer Lowe among them, for what the ship's log described as 'guard duties during Czech occupation of Vladivostok.'

The attack was well coordinated and swiftly executed and during the morning there was little bloodshed beyond a few shots exchanged and a comparative handful of deaths and injuries. The Red Guards, overwhelmed by the numbers of well-trained Czechs, stood little chance of resistance. In the afternoon there was a brief rally near the waterfront where longshoremen, stevedores and coal-heavers – the working men of the proletariat – made their way to the Red Staff building and barricaded themselves in with rifles at the ready. They kept up their fire until nightfall when under cover of darkness the Czechs were able to lodge an incendiary bomb through a window of the building; the ensuing blaze forced the last pocket of resistance out into the streets, their hands raised in surrender. The dockworkers – *gruzckiki* (longshoremen) – were promptly shot, beaten or taken prisoner.

Elsewhere in the city, even as the last resistance was being over-whelmed, the mood was one of celebration. The Red Flag was hauled down and replaced by the Tsar's flag at Bolshevik headquarters. The cry went up 'The Soviet has fallen', and in the streets men exchanged the words as if, recorded Albert Rhys Williams bitterly,

they were 'an Easter greeting'. From his third storey vantage point
Williams watched along the length of the thoroughfare Svetlanskaya,
which was 'boiling now like a cauldron. This street, which twenty
minutes earlier had been so placid in the shining morning sun, is
now a riot of people and colour and sound. Blue-jacketed Japs in
white puttees, English marines with the Union Jack, khaki-clad
Czechs, with green and white, marching and counter-marching, cut
currents thru the eddying throng, each moment growing greater.'[98]
Celebrations continued into the night, with lights blazing and music
played loud and long in homes and restaurants, spilling out into the
summer night. Church bells rang, and from the cruisers in the harbour came the call of bugles.

Lowe had work to do. While around him cheers went up for the
men in Allied uniform, he was assigned to escort Bolshevik prisoners. That evening at 8 p.m. the *Suffolk* withdrew all the small arms
companies except for the consular guard. There had not been any
casualties, or even serious injuries, among the British. Searchlights
were burned as the wharfs were searched and the port guns were at
night defence stations.[99]

A proclamation was issued by the Czech, British, American,
Japanese and Chinese representatives in Vladivostok declaring
the area 'under the temporary protection of the Allied Powers…
for its defence against dangers internal and external'. Numbers of
wounded Czechs and Russians were taken on board the *Suffolk* for
treatment. During the next few weeks the Russian anti-Bolshevik
groups coalesced under the leadership of Admiral Kolchak, forming
a government at Omsk that covered geographic territory over half
of Russia, setting the scene for the civil war proper between Reds
and Whites.

The action swiftly shifted elsewhere, and the *Suffolk*'s men settled
once more into routine patterns of drill, cleaning and painting the
ship, and washing and mending clothes. During the year he spent
in Vladivostok, Lowe spent enough time ashore in the company of
locals to gain a proficiency in their language that went beyond the
odd word or phrase. As Vladivostok calmed, Lowe and his fellow
officers were even able to go deer hunting.

In July there was a reminder of how savage the interior fighting
had been. In the Ussuri district a Dr Teusler found the bodies of
Czech soldiers mutilated on the battlefield, tongues cut out, heads
split and genitalia removed. Four of the disfigured corpses were

brought to Vladivostok for an official investigation, attended by one of the *Suffolk's* doctors. A verdict was reached of injuries inflicted before death.[100]

News of the end of the war to end wars came slowly to Siberia. On 10 November, the master-at-arms recorded in his diary: 'Very cold. Divine service. Very good telegrams received.' The ship's complement still had not heard anything by the following day – Armistice Day itself – and after wiring a query spent their time 'waiting reply anxiously'.

The response came on 12 November: 'A lovely sunny day. Received telegram, that hostilities ceased at 5 am GMT yesterday. Great rejoicing at the news received.'[101]

The ship was dressed the next day. Celebrations continued to 15 November, when there was a parade of Allied troops in Vladivostok. Three companies from the *Suffolk* and her band represented the cruiser and mingled with Americans, Chinese, Japanese, Russians, Czechs, Italians and Canadians.

Then came the waiting. Ever expectant of orders home, the *Suffolk's* men were already heading deep into their second Siberian winter. Lowe was photographed on the ship's deck almost buried in a heavy fur coat and hat, the ship's dog Puppsie cradled in his arms. Finally came news that the cruiser was to be relieved by a sister ship and on 3 January 1919 a farewell concert was given at the YMCA building by the HMS *Suffolk* band, with combined Czech and American musical support. At 10.15 a.m. the next day HMS *Kent* entered harbour.

Like the *Suffolk* the year before, *Kent* had experienced severe gales that caused icicles to hang from yards, rigging and boats. The *Suffolk's* crew, who had spent many watches shovelling snow from her own upper decks, were relieved to see the commodore's broad pennant hauled down and final preparations made for their departure.

On 7 January the *Suffolk* cast off at last, bound for Yokohama. The Czech band played something suitably melancholic ashore and the *Brooklyn* sounded her brasses. From other ships in the harbour came a tremendous cacophony of cheers. The men on board were elated with the promise that they would soon be setting course for England. *Suffolk* departed Vladivostok in gently falling snow that blurred the harsh lines of the warships.

Although prospects for Kolchak and the Allied forces still seemed bright when the *Suffolk* finished her duties there, 1919 was to bring about a turnaround in their fortunes. Gradually the Allies withdrew, the British departing in the winter of 1919–20. Kolchak was eventually defeated by the 3rd and 5th Red Armies on 8 January 1920 at Krasnoyarsk. Captured by the Bolsheviks, he was executed on 7 February 1920. Neither the Czechs, Americans or Japanese, who still had a presence in Vladivostok, attempted to save their former ally. The Czechoslovaks and an American hospital in Vladivostok were evacuated in March 1920 and the last American troops had left by April 1920. The Japanese eventually bowed to pressure to withdraw brought to bear by the Americans at the July 1921 Washington Conference.

The intervention had proved a costly error and would long have a souring effect on relations between the fledgling USSR and the Allied powers. Public opinion, without the justification that it was necessary to support the war effort and with increasing social unrest in Britain, had turned against intervention. Lowe, like so many of those at all levels of the Navy and government, questioned the wisdom of foreign powers involving themselves in Russia's internal affairs. While it is unlikely Lowe had any sympathy for the Bolshevik cause, as the civil war had progressed the Allies had come to the realisation that there was little distinction in the brutality of tactics employed by both the Red and White armies.

It was a long way home. Even after leaving Vladivostok, *Suffolk* was assigned duties that kept her in the Far East for a few months yet. They spent a week in Yokohama, where the press reported that her crew of 720 were 'ready for a fight or frolic, but with a decided inclination to the latter just now'. The British expatriate community gave them a warm welcome.

Next call was Singapore, where the men and the well-worked ship's band were landed in February as a guard of honour to celebrate its 100th anniversary as a British colony. The crew attended the unveiling of a statue of Sir Stamford Raffles, and there was a gala display of fireworks on the racecourse.

The ship underwent a general refit in Hong Kong during the second half of that month, after which she was ordered to Shanghai. Arriving in March, some of the *Suffolk*'s ABs were detailed to guard Germans POWs aboard the SS *Novena*. Lowe, photographing the ship, referred to 'Huns' on board.

Finally, on 16 April – Ellen Lowe's birthday – the *Suffolk* turned for home. It was seven years after the *Titanic* and the world had changed out of all recognition.

During the course of his war service Lowe came to own a small statuette, taken from the notorious German raider *Emden*. It was probably originally snatched by one from HMAS *Sydney*, the Australian vessel that brought an end to the *Emden*'s daring and destructive career. The *Sydney*, accompanied by a submarine squadron, had been in Aden when the *Suffolk* arrived there on her homeward voyage. Lowe had an opportunity to exchange souvenirs since the *Suffolk* was stuffed with many a memento of the Russian campaign in the form of Bolshevik swords, medals, bits of revolutionary ribbon, and pillows made of pieces of cloth of gold.

Suffolk sailed through the Suez Canal, troops at Kantara shouting out questions, asking when they too would be relieved. They also passed troopships heading home in the opposite direction with ANZAC soldiers in distinctive slouch hats. Everyone was anxious for the long trick to be over.

On 25 May the *Suffolk* sighted the Rock of Gibraltar. Three days later the Lizard came into view. By 7 p.m. she was in Plymouth. And suddenly they were home.

Lowe was reunited with Nellie and two children he hardly knew. On 17 June he took the family to Barmouth, where for the next three months they enjoyed an extended holiday at Penrallt. It was a post-war summer idyll, as Lowe photographed Nellie, dark-haired Josie and 'The Little Man', his name for Harold junior, picnicking, swimming, larking on the beach and sailing in the Bay. The lieutenant had served faithfully and well, although no special opportunities had come his way and it is doubtful that he was ever called upon to fire a shot in anger. Lowe returned to Colwyn Bay, where he was in due course issued with one of the certificates issued to all residents who had done their duty. Signed by the chairman of the Colwyn Bay Urban District Council, it recorded high appreciation of services rendered to King and Country during the Great War:

> It was by the cheerful courage and steadfast endurance of Sailors, Soldiers and Airmen in the hour of the world's peril that Victory crowned the cause of Justice and Liberty.
>
> We salute you as one that hath done valiantly.

CHAPTER 14

FAMILIES IN DECLINE

The White Star Line, like the rest of the merchant marine, had taken a heavy beating. Under the terms finally ending the conflict it would receive some compensation, most notably Germany's uncompleted *Bismarck*. This vessel, renamed the *Majestic* in due course, was intended as compensation for the loss of the *Titanic*'s sister ship *Britannic*, which went down to a mine off Greece while serving as a hospital vessel.

Lowe's first berth after the war would not, however, be with a White Star Line vessel. Instead, he signed aboard Frederick Leyland & Co.'s SS *Turcoman* on 25 November 1919. Such exchanges of officers were not uncommon among International Mercantile Marine lines and the reallocation of men and even ships between services took place as suited the conglomerate. Boxhall was another to find the *Turcoman* one of his earliest post-war positions.

On his next voyage, 9 January 1920, Lowe sailed from Liverpool on the *Cedric* as her second officer. For the first time since the *Titanic* disaster eight years before, Lowe was back on the North Atlantic passenger run and, on 21 January, the ship called at New York. It was a place invested with many memories for Lowe, not all of them pleasant. He was on *Cedric* into February, sailing again from Liverpool on 16 February and arriving in New York on the 28th of the month. Doing back-to-back voyages on her into April 1920 he seems to have felt rather an affection for the old vessel and in March drew a pen and ink sketch of her for a relative, Jane Lowe Whitehouse.

Lowe was not the only old *Titanic* man to sail on the *Cedric* in the immediate post-war years. Demobilised earlier than Harold Lowe, a berth as second officer of the *Cedric* had marked Joseph Boxhall's return to the merchant service on 16 May 1919. He made several crossings with the old ship throughout the second half of 1919. The similarity in Boxhall and Lowe's post-war careers, first seen in their postings to the *Turcoman* and *Cedric*, resolved into a pattern throughout the remainder of Lowe's career in the 1920s. They served aboard the same ships within relatively short periods of each other, in positions of approximately equal seniority.

Later that year, in August of 1920, Lowe signed on as first officer of the SS *Dominion* of the Dominion Line, another International Mercantile Marine ship. It was the beginning of his association with Canada, one which would be of importance throughout the remainder of his working life. White Star's service ran from Liverpool to Quebec and Montreal. In winter, when the St Laurence River was icebound and ships could not pass up to Quebec and Montreal, the Canadian service terminated in Halifax. Lowe was always rather drawn to frontiers and wild, elemental places, be it the sea or the mountains of New Zealand, and Canada captured his imagination as it did that of his literary hero, Robert Service. Cities were never his sphere, but the *Dominion* also called at New York on 25 October 1920. Irish leader Eamon de Valera, arriving in Manhattan in June 1919 on the *Lapland*, found it a city of 'straw hats and sunshine' basking in the brilliance of the first post-war summer. It was the dawning of the American Age.

A number of factors in the interwar period combined to alter the nature of the passenger trade. Most significant among these was the decline in the immigration that had been such a pre-war staple of the shipping companies, brought about by American legislative restrictions on immigration. New markets had to be found, and the White Star Line led the way in the development of tourist class. Passenger areas formerly utilised for steerage were now converted for use by what was newly marketed as the 'tourist third cabin', many of them Americans travelling abroad on a budget. The post-1919 Prohibition laws of the 1920s also added to the appeal of transatlantic travel, as it allowed thirsty Americans to indulge in the tipples that were banned for them ashore. Not all the old seamen would take to the new, tourist-orientated style of ocean travel that became popular in the 1920s. Joseph Boxhall, a sailor of the old school like his father before him, disliked it, preferring the days before the liners took to cruising.

An advantage in the Atlantic run was the opportunity it afforded Lowe to spend more time at home with his young family. In their earliest years he had naturally been a remote figure, even a rumour, and it would be recalled by Harold Junior that he did not have a close relationship with his father until at least the age of six.

Although always 'kind and fair', the years away at war had cre-
ated a certain distance, yet Josie and Harold were now able to see
more of their daddy during his spells ashore. Shore time threatened
to become a permanent grounding. The North Atlantic passenger
trade was undergoing significant change, with the decline in emi-
gration to North America affecting the industry.

It made sense for Lowe, never a company yes-man, to take steps
to broaden his opportunities for possible employment. He opted to
embrace Freemasonry and on 13 May 1921 Brother Harold Godfrey
Lowe was initiated into the St Trillo Lodge. He was passed by the
members that October and entered the ranks the following January.

Lowe's involvement in the Brotherhood did not extend to
seeking a position of seniority. Lodge records show he never held
office from the time of his initiation until his death. But it was an
organisation ideally suited to a seaman who could stay in his chosen
profession, with social contacts all over the world.

Social isolation does not seem to have been a problem for Lowe
and references to some of the close relationships he cultivated
during his life debunk any ideas of him being a 'loner'. He tended
to cultivate fewer, deeper friendships rather than a wider circle of
friends, but some of these were profound and afforded him social
contact when far from home. What is perhaps notable is the range
of friends Lowe had, drawn from an interesting social cross section. A long stint of service on the Canadian run in the mid-1920s
provided an opportunity for Lowe to form friendships in ports he
called at frequently. Among those he counted in his close circle of
'pals' was a Montreal firefighter; this contact proved useful when
Lowe needed red paint to provide the background to the White
Star burgee when he used the device on some of his handiwork,
including a napkin ring he carved. From local railway station
attendants to Canadian firemen, social boundaries and occupations
meant little to him.

He resumed his friendship with Harry Pearce, interrupted by the
war, and was introduced to his son, Henry 'Bobby' Pearce, one of the
most remarkable of Australia's Olympic athletes. Bobby Pearce won
back-to-back Olympic titles in 1928 and 1932 while still compet-
ing as an amateur, the only pre-Second World War singles sculler
to achieve such a feat and the first Australian Olympic athlete to
win successive gold medals. After his second successful Olympics he
turned professional and went on to win the world title. A formidable

athlete, there was a chivalrous quality to his competitive sportsman-
ship. A story still related in rowing circles today concerns a race in
which he was so far out ahead of his nearest rival that he could
afford to pull up to let a mother and her trail of ducklings cross the
river in front of him. He went on to win the race.

In the parlance of the time, Harry and Lowe were 'great pals',
spending time together in Australia when Harold's voyages took him
to the southern continent. They also exchanged gifts, including a silver
cigar case given to Lowe and inscribed 'From One Pal to Another'.[102]
His photographs show father and son training on Penrith lakes and
also in their rowing gear in what appears to be their back yard, with
washing on the line and the glare of an antipodean sun.

Lowe's admiration for Pearce as both a friend and an athlete
reflected his own enthusiasm for physical prowess. Not always a team
player in any sense of the word, he relished individualistic sports.
Shooting and fishing had long been his passions, and he indulged
them whenever possible. So proficient was he with firearms that he
was offered the chance to compete for the King's Prize at the Imperial
Meeting, the most prestigious rifle-shooting event in England held
each July at Bisley in Surrey. His career demands made such participa-
tion impossible, but he cherished the honour of the invitation.

Following his five voyages in the *Dominion* as her first officer, in
April 1921 Lowe found himself abruptly on the beach, forced on
to extended leave on half pay due to lack of available work. For
just over a year, from 8 April 1921 to 13 May 1922, he found little
else to do but spend time with his family and on personal interests.
Lowe spent the time working on projects such as the construction
of a scale model of a Nova Scotian fishing boat, remembered with
pride as having 'sailed beautifully' when completed. Lowe named
the vessel *Half Pay*. He also worked to construct a duck-punt for
wild-fowling and spear fishing.

It was with no inconsiderable relief that in May 1922 Lowe joined
the *Gallic* as chief officer, and for the next six voyages (and one short
coasting trip to Hamburg) he sailed to Australia and New Zealand.
Lowe's attainment of chief officer of the *Gallic* was the highest rank
he would ever achieve in the Merchant Marine.

In 1923 he made the newspapers again; but in a much more mundane way than through his *Titanic* experiences. He had caught two
specimen kingfish in Australia and the *Poverty Bay Herald* carried
a photo of Lowe standing beside his catch, pipe in hand. A framed

clipping of the article, complete with a section of fishing line, was presented to the Seaman's Mission in Barmouth where it still hangs on the wall.

There was other recognition to come, and on and the day before his forty-first birthday, in November 1923, he was finally awarded the rank of commander RNR. It was formal recognition of the service he had given the Navy and its reserve forces over many years, and he used the rank of 'Commander' with pride for the remainder of his life.

Lowe continued to alternate between the Australian and Canadian runs for the remainder of his career, with only occasional forays to the United States. By now his younger brother, Edward, who had followed Harold's example by joining the merchant service, was also making a career at sea. Edward was thirty-three years old and living in Wellington, New Zealand, in 1927 when he joined the SS *Waitemata* for yet another workaday voyage. The other Officer Lowe happened to be working this voyage as an Able Seaman, a trifle unusually. It may be that a rusty unfamiliarity with deck work played a role in his being lost overboard on 11 March. The body was never recovered.

Of all the possibilities that had run through his mind, that of the sea claiming a second brother did not remotely feature. Instead of a tragedy at home in Wales, it was yet another agony of salt tears and salt water.

The march of time now brought another loss to the Lowe family. The artist and drinker George Edward Lowe, Harold's father, had long been suffering from chronic inflammation of the kidneys. He passed away in November 1928, watched over by Artie, the one son who never left Barmouth. George was eighty-one years old and had survived his wife and two of his sons. He was interred in the churchyard of St Mary's in the hills above Barmouth. The headstone commemorated not only him but also his wife Harriet and name-sake George, deceased so many years before, with further mention of Edward and the longitude and latitude in which he had been lost.

Lowe's relationship with his father had been complex to begin with but had long since reached a loving accommodation. George Lowe's personal weaknesses had helped shape his son's outlook and character but while Harold had fled from his father's attempts to control his destiny, in the end it was to Barmouth that he had

returned. When Lowe stepped off the *Adriatic*, back from the jaws of
death in 1912, George had been there to meet him.

Lowe, once the runaway, was now the family patriarch. He organised his father's funeral, down to details such as lending money to his
siblings to buy appropriate suits and flowers. According to the terms
of the will he took charge of the sale of Penrallt, and managed both
lawyers and the family interests. His customary bluntness did not
always endear him to the family lawyers. 'From his recent attitude
towards our Firm,' they wrote in offence to his legal representatives, 'it
is evident that he does not appreciate the way in which we have met
him...' Finally, though, the differences were settled and Penrallt sold.

There was another curtain drawn across a part of Lowe's life
around this time. His long service with the Reserves finally came to
an end on his forty-fifth birthday in 1927. There had already been
official recognition by both the government and the White Star Line
(the latter not averse to the good publicity and cachet of having
RNR men in its ranks) for his long-standing service in the reserves
in the form of the Reserve Decoration for long and efficient service. A special ceremony was organised at Oceanic Chambers and
Commodore C.A. Bartlett, in the presence of a number of RNR
officers, presented the decoration to Lowe.

That it meant a great deal to him is indicated by the clippings he
kept about the presentation, which contained references to both his
White Star Line career and a précis of his war service. It was a form
of acknowledgement from his peers for the service to his country. He
had only ever desired 'three gongs': i.e. the British War Medal 1914–18,
the Victory Medal (Inter Allied War Medal), and 'one other'. [103] That
one other was the Royal Naval Reserve Decoration, an oval medal
suspended on a plain dark-green ribbon, awarded for fifteen years'
continuous service: 'He was rather proud of that one.' [104]

Also in recognition of the service he had rendered to his country,
he was retired at the rank of lieutenant commander.

Lowe's merchant marine career continued on the Australian run,
much longer voyages than the service to North America. It was an
event of some excitement for his children therefore when daddy finally
came home every several months and a tremendous sense of antici-
pation that Harold Junior would remember forever. One can easily
imagine Josie and young Harold, well scrubbed and dressed in their
best, ready to greet their father at the garden gate of Bryn Mostyn,
while ever eager to see what he had brought them from overseas.

Harold Jr remembered a man who was extremely self-controlled, despite the picture painted by Daisy Minahan. He recalled his father as tolerant and unhurried. 'As a boy I must have, not infrequently, given him cause for annoyance but he never raised his hand to me in anger nor for that matter did he chastise me verbally in heat or impatience.' He held his officer father in 'awe and respect, blended with affection.'

The young Harold kept a letter from his father, written on 22 September 1928 on board the *Doric*, another White Star liner, and taken off at Belfast. Lowe wrote to his son:

Dear Harold,
Many thanks for your unsuspected parcel. It was a very nice thought of yours, but I regret to state that you have not quite understood me, & besides you have spent far too much money, which I must refund when I return.

The greatest pleasure you can give both your mother & myself is to try to be an ordinary boy, (I do not mean that I want you to be unnaturally good) & try sometimes to be quick & obedient, so as to give us positive proof that you appreciate our kindnesses, then you will be a happy boy, & to be happy is to be contented in your own mind & if you go on trying, you will grow to be a big, happy, & contented man, & you will radiate happiness wherever you go, & everyone will love & like you, which is about the greatest possession a man can have.

Just read this letter over carefully, then keep & study what it contains. Afterwards re-read it, & perhaps you will get the idea, I have tried to convey to you.

You seem to be naughty (in spite of yourself & go off into dreamland without you yourself knowing it, you will have to exercise quite a lot of your will-power & I am convinced that you can easily manage it if you only try).

Don't forget to try to learn all you can, in school, as you have quite a lot of exams to pass yet.

Again thanking you for your very nice present which was quite a surprise to me.

With fond love,
Your loving father,
Dadds

P.S. I hope we will have another days shooting when I return.

It is intriguing that Lowe, an individualist who had always followed his own path, should place such an emphasis on the approbation of others. Would the Harold Godfrey Lowe of the early years have cared so much to have others 'like and love' him that he would regard it as 'the greatest possession' a man could have? Time and experience had wrought their changes, and softened – though never entirely smoothed out – some of the edges.

His admonition to his son about the need to exercise willpower in order to avoid both naughtiness and daydreaming (the latter evidently something of a sin in the eyes of the practical Harold Lowe) ring a thoroughly conventional note at a time when self-discipline was a prized quality, but in Lowe's case it was more than a platitude. Self-discipline was a quality he had worked at personally his entire life.

It seems Lowe was determined to be a steadying influence in his son's life, quite different from his own upbringing. Knowing and regretting that he could not be there in person more often to guide his son, he did his best in correspondence.

Lowe once tried to spectacularly indulge his children. In an echo of the days when he collected apes for the zoos of Europe, aided and abetted by Harry Pearce, he made a daring effort to acquire a koala on one of his trips to Australia. Taronga Zoo in Sydney seemed the logical place, but the quarantine and export regulations defeated the idea, to Harold Jr's lasting disappointment once he found out.

As the children became older, Lowe was able to introduce them to his own passions of boating, fishing and shooting. Lowe would never own a car or learn to drive; perhaps he regarded it as 'landlubber navigation'. He instead hired several boatmen, with whom he would converse in Welsh. His own children never learned the language but Lowe retained the fluency he had developed in his own childhood. Occasionally his Welsh dropped into Russian, a legacy of his time in Vladivostok, one that was perfectly perplexing to the hands he took on.

At least one incident with Harold Jr struck a resonance with Lowe's own childhood and reminded him that he was growing old. At the age of twelve, young Harold, who shared his father's love of the sea and ships, took a sailing dinghy out under potentially dangerous weather conditions. On his return, he found his father waiting. Lowe first took the boy to task for his rashness, knowing all too well the consequences of imprudence at sea. Later he confessed that he too had done much the same thing when about the same age.

As he grew up, Harold Jr was better able to assess his father's character and temperament. His observations provide a contrast to popular perceptions of Lowe as overly excitable and short tempered. 'He could become enthusiastic, yes, and he had a great sense of humour, but excited to the point of any reduction of self-control, no!' The father that Harold knew was quite the opposite, and he would offer the phrases 'self contained' and 'self possessed' in description. Towards the end of his life, he commented: 'My father was one of the most even-tempered men I have ever met.'[105]

Yet his propensity for strong language did not abate with time, and would even enter family tradition. Janet Lowe, member of a distant branch of the Lowes, remarked on the family recollection that: 'His manners were those of a perfect Victorian gentleman – with language littered with high seas invective.' Nor was she the only one to comment on his vivid use of invective. Barbara Whitehouse, a young visiting relation, was wide-eyed at his use of language, in spite of the fact that her father and uncle were also merchant officers.[106]

If his language was as it had always been, Lowe remained idiosyncratic in dress. When meeting anyone or performing official duties, he was always immaculately turned out. On Sundays especially, he would put on a good suit for church and allow himself a lily of the valley, rather than the more conventional rose or carnation. Personal recreation was a different matter. He wore 'whatever mode of dress he considered to be most suitable rather than what was normally accepted.' Although he never had any interest in horse riding, Lowe adopted jodhpurs as part of both his boating ensemble, and even as ordinary daywear. What other people thought of it was of no consequence to him whatever.[107]

The Canadian run beckoned once more, and he was assigned to the newest – if one of the least pleasing – White Star Line vessels, the *Laurentic*, shortly after her 1927 maiden voyage. A few months later, on 27 July 1928, Lowe joined another of the former White-Star Dominion ships (changed to 'White Star (Canadian Services)' in 1925), this time as second officer of the *Doric*. The *Doric* was a twin-screw with single-reduction geared turbines, and was the only pure turbine ship ever built for White Star. Once again the run was Liverpool to Quebec and Montreal, via Belfast and Glasgow. He was promoted on board her to first officer, but she was to be his last ship.

It was readily apparent to Lowe in these final years of his career that he would never achieve promotion beyond senior officer and that top-of-the-line ships like the *Olympic* and *Majestic* would remain

unattainable. His role as a bridge officer on the *Titanic*, the most notorious sea disaster of all time, was almost certainly a factor in this career
stagnation. Nor was he alone in this; of the four surviving officers, all
of whom had once been considered so promising as to be appointed
to the most luxurious ship in the world on her maiden voyage, none
would ever achieve a command in the merchant service.

Lightoller directly attributed his lack of promotion to command
to the White Star Line's desire not have those associated with the
disaster in command of other ships. While the company never said as
much, he was simply allowed to languish as chief officer of the *Celtic*.
Finally, on 14 February 1920, his resignation took effect. All that was
said to the former second officer of the *Titanic* as he handed in his
notice was, 'Oh, you are leaving us, are you. Well, Goodbye.'

Pitman had 'voluntarily' surrendered his certificate in 1913 when
new regulations on colour blindness obligated him to do so. Having
known no other career than the sea, he took up duties as purser
– a capacity in which he served until retirement in 1949, having
remained at sea longer than any of his ex-*Titanic* colleagues. He even
served briefly as an assistant purser on board the *Olympic*.

Boxhall found himself in much the same position as Lowe, even
to the point of both serving in the same vessels at the same rank in
swift succession. Boxhall did manage a stint as first officer of the
four-stacker *Aquitania* in the 1930s but would rise no further.

While Lightoller was adamant that the *Titanic* caused his lack of
advancement, Lowe suspected another factor in his own case. In the
world of shipping, as in industry, preferment could often be the result
of cronyism rather than ability. Lowe noted that many of his colleagues
obtained their promotions by taking a certain senior White Star figure
out to dinner and 'plying him with gin'. The idea was abhorrent to Lowe,
both morally and as an adamant abstainer and he refused to indulge.

The promise of the spring of 1912, when he had been assigned to
the pride and joy of the line, must have seemed unimaginably distant
by 1930. There were other disappointments. The Wall Street Crash
of 1929 was a devastating blow to Lowe. From his earliest days in
sail he had managed his funds carefully, a habit retained throughout
his life. But as the world entered the Great Depression and financial
institutions failed, luckless Lowe was among those who lost nearly
all their savings. In particular a mining investment turned sour. The
impact of this loss, at a time when he was already frustrated by his
lack of promotion, was savage.

The family was by no means destitute; Nellie's father was comfortably off, but the situation must have demoralising and demeaning to one who had always been so careful with his finances. In these waning years of his career he was promoted to first officer of the *Doric*. Perhaps he also already had a sense of his own time running out. A family history of hypertension and strokes meant that he carried within him a ticking genetic time bomb; his mother and her father had both succumbed to strokes. The indications were that Lowe was never destined to live a long life. The first inklings of health problems were already apparent by 1930, and he had been obliged to take a leave of absence from the *Doric* due to illness.

Nellie's father died from pneumonia in May 1931. William Whitehouse had been nursed for years by his daughter, and his passing was a great blow. Lowe supported his wife through the burden of her loss and dutifully reported the death to the registry office. It must have been with mixed feelings that they contemplated what the loss of Nellie's father meant for them, as the bequests to his daughter rescued their financial position.

Harold Lowe had now finally had enough. Even if he regretted the quiet end to a career he had invested so much in, he tendered his resignation to the White Star Line. We do not know if he, like Lightoller, was met with an off-hand phrase in response to his notice, but as the company had acknowledged his service in other spheres at the Reserve Decoration ceremony held in his honour, and the disaster was a long-ago affair from his days as a junior officer, largely eclipsed by many years of service since in the interwar period, it is likely that he received something more in the way of acknowledgement.

Including those years he spent in RNR service, Lowe had been with the grand old company for twenty years. Ironically, White Star itself would not see out the 1930s as an independent entity, merging with rival Cunard in order to ride out the worldwide Depression.

By August 1931 the Lowes sold up in Colwyn Bay and moved to nearby Deganwy. Now, for the first time, Harold Lowe had his own home, rather than the boarding houses and shore addresses with family that had been his lot since he had first gone to sea. It was purchased, however, in Nellie's name. Freed from the drowning embrace of the White Star Line, Lowe announced that he intended to enjoy 'ten years of fishing and shooting before I am too old to do so.'

CHAPTER 15

'BEFORE I'M TOO OLD'

Deganwy is a pleasant place for any seaman to bury the anchor. Visitors still stroll along the promenade, past the bathing huts along the strip of beach, while the Conway River endlessly flows and ebbs with the tides. Across the river from the small town lie the romantic ruins of Conway Castle, Edward I's thirteenth-century edifice.

The smell of the tobacco smoke from Harold Lowe's pipe lingered long in his house in Deganwy, even for many years after Lowe himself was gone. But he was determined to enjoy the time left to him in his retirement, and that still meant boats and the sea.

Lowe was no technological troglodyte, as his acquisition of a motorboat, still a comparatively new innovation for small private recreational craft, attested. Named *Cariad*, Welsh for 'sweetheart', she was 20ft long with a half cabin and a square transom. He used her for trawling or handline fishing in the estuary and Colwyn Bay. In winter he took her upriver for occasional wild-fowling expeditions, accompanied by his Welsh terrier, Gyp.

There were echoes of childhood spent on the shores of the Mawddach, and now his son was experiencing a similar idyll and love of seacraft. One day when Harold Jr was assisting him in painting the boat, Lowe suddenly presented him with a peaked cap, one with the White Star Line burgee in a wreath of laurel. It was, he told the lad, the very cap he was wearing on the night the *Titanic* went down.

Tucked away somewhere else were the tunic buttons worn then, save for the one he long ago sent to Sheriff Joe Bayliss. In his collection of firearms lay the Browning automatic he had fired. He showed it to his children, telling them something of its history. All were part of a story they heard from their father only in fragments: the reason for a gold sovereign on his watch chain; the maritime equipment Rene Harris had given him; the gun with its gaping barrel; how he had fired it; the reasons he waited to return for survivors. These stories were reluctantly given. Even as a boy, Harold Jr recognised that the recollections were clouded by an unspoken pain. He asked his mother about it, and Nellie, who had been through the aftermath, explained with almost equal reticence that, 'he never talks about it'.

Others did, perpetuating many myths. In April 1932, on the twentieth anniversary of the sinking, Rene Harris wrote a highly coloured article for *Liberty* magazine. She had come far since Lowe last saw her in New York. She had faced both the loss of her husband Henry and the financial mess he left behind with courage and acumen, building up a theatrical empire. It ended in 1929 with the stock market crash.

The intervening years had not dimmed her recollection or admiration for Lowe. She made a special point of mentioning in her article the man she dubbed the 'Real Hero' of the night: 'If by some freak of circumstance Fifth Officer Lowe should read these lines, he will know that through all the years he has stood out in my memory as one of the finest men it has been my privilege to meet.' Harris would have been gratified to know that the words did indeed reach Lowe in far away North Wales. Friends in America sent the magazine to him and he was evidently very pleased to receive it, placing it among his personal papers. Reconnecting with Harris, the two exchanged Christmas cards.

Also among his papers was a reprint of Charlotte Collyer's 1912 article about the disaster. It came to him courtesy of Collyer's daughter Marjorie, who as a small girl had begged Lowe not to 'shoot the poor man' who had entered a lifeboat. Now married to a mechanic named Roy Dutton and living in Chilworth, Surrey, Marjorie wrote to Lowe at Christmas 1935 to say that as his name was mentioned in her mother's article several times; she wondered if he would care to accept a copy.

Marjorie found her way into Lowe's address book with the annotation '*Titanic*' beside it, thus joining a handful of survivor names and details that appear in his records. As Marjorie made reference to Lowe's family in the note, it appears Lowe at least exchanged Christmas cards and notes with some of the 'club' of April 1912.

Although retired, he was to have another near-miss with the sea, this time in circumstances the ageing officer found quite humiliating. On 19 November 1937, on the threshold of his fifty-fifth birthday, he and his friend William Parry, a railway clerk, were taking a dinghy out to Lowe's 30ft, half-cabined motorboat *Pirate*. Both sea and wind were rough, and while Parry managed to step onto *Pirate*,

Lowe was caught by a sudden gust of wind. He lost his footing and fell. Immediately his knee-high boots began filling with water. Lowe, who as a boy had swum half a mile to shore while fully dressed, now faced an inglorious end. His strength was failing as he struggled in the freezing water. He could feel himself beginning to sink.

Fortunately his companion had enough presence of mind to grab Lowe's coat collar. William Parry hauled him head-first out of the water and then dragged him towards the boat. Lowe, exhausted, was saved from drowning. Parry recovered his own strength, pulled Lowe in, then took him home.

The incident was both frightening and a stunning blow to Lowe's self-image. He was always a man who had taken considerable pride in his skills as a boatman. It was also a reminder of the brothers he had lost, particularly in its similarity to the death of George Jr in an accident now forty-three years before. But worse was the story's humiliating sequel. The *Liverpool Echo* ran an article under the headline '*Titanic* Survivor Rescued – Fell into River at Deganwy.' Once again, the *Titanic* and the media had intruded into his life in a most unwelcome manner. It was bad enough that the accident had befallen him, worse still that it had been made so public.

For a while he stayed on land. He could spend hours shuttered away in his workshop in the back garden, developing his talent for handicrafts, woodwork and joinery. Surrounded by tins of paint and linseed oil that had 'fallen off the back of a ship,' he also had a First World War trench-telescope mounted on the wall, focused on the church clock for a quick check of the time.

Lowe took the unusual step of going into local politics. He was elected unopposed in the Deganwy Ward of Conwy Borough Council in November 1932. But he was reluctant to take his involvement beyond the position of councillor and when heavily pressured by colleagues to run for mayor, simply declined, commenting that having been asked was sufficient honour for him.

He later told his son that a strong deterrent was the publicity that would have accompanied the position if his nomination was successful. While possessed of many outstanding leadership qualities that were recognised by others, Lowe still balked at the glare of public scrutiny.

Lowe's two terms on the council saw an ambitious drive for infrastructure and improved amenities in Deganwy. The sea wall

was extended, behind which the sand dunes were levelled and con-
creted, making a promenade walk. New bathing cubicles were also
erected, along with refreshment kiosks, public conveniences and a
children's paddling pool.

He was chairman of the Bridge Committee when Prime Minister
Lloyd George opened the new Civic Centre in 1937. The wily old
man, who had represented the area for half a century, praised the
initiative of the local authority. 'I am glad to see the fine courage –
and even audacity – of the Conwy councillors in doing the right
thing,' enthused the 'Welsh Wizard'. Lowe sat on the dais in characteristic cross-armed posture while the man also dubbed the 'Welsh
Windbag' held forth.

Council minutes show Lowe could become impatient when
meetings became bogged down in bureaucracy and he would move
or second a motion in order to get matters moving. Soon he had
drafted in his wife in support. Nellie became involved in civic
duties, heading committees that supported the council's work. By
the time Lowe retired at the end of his second term in 1938, he
had established a record of diligence. His attendance at council and
committee meetings surpassed that of most of his colleagues.

Strict regulation was noted among his contemporaries as an
outstanding characteristic of the Lowe household. The habit of command had been grown in both the Navy and Merchant Marine, and
he translated it to his shore life. Even the family pets were exceptionally well disciplined, as Lowe demonstrated to visitors. He would put
a piece of food on the head of his dog Gyp when he begged at the
table. The Welsh terrier then sat motionless, ignoring the temptation,
until permitted by his master to eat the titbit. On one occasion Lowe
placed a piece of pie on the dog's head and forgot about it, until the
dog eventually found a way of reminding him.

The Depression years passed more comfortably for the Lowes than
for most, with Nellie's inheritance enough to keep them ensconced
in middle-class existence. Their area also survived the prolonged economic trough comparatively well, especially when compared to the
sufferings of heavily industrialised North Wales. Visitors to the Lowes
remembered the hospitality and warmth of Nellie and Josie, who had
much of her mother's temperament and view of life. Harold's tongue
was as sharp as ever, as relatives on the Lowe/Whitehouse side of the
family, Bewsher Whitehouse and Bernard Harrison, would note with

amusement. The two thought a good deal of him, respect borne of a similar merchant and RNR background, and they were certainly no strangers themselves to the strong language in seamen that was proverbial. However, even by their standards Lowe's use of expletives was exceptional. In spite of this, Lowe had managed to shape himself into a self-described 'pillar of the community', a churchwarden who took on the role of prominent local citizen. Never quite absolutely conventional, when passing the collection plate he would tease the congregation by asking for the traditional tithe. They may have thought he was serious.

Lowe had achieved respect and standing in his community, his own small world. But beyond the holidaymakers on the Conwy River, the Welsh hills and the sea, he continued to take an interest in wider events, the activities of 'his' Bolsheviks especially, and he cannot have failed to watch of the rise of fascism in opposition to international communism.

No doubt he also had a keen consciousness of the Far East and a remark he made to his son about the 'treacherous' Japanese was against a background of Japanese imperialism in the 1930s. His respect for the Chinese had dated from his early days at sea, and the Japanese invasion of Manchuria and atrocities such as the Rape of Nanking, would surely have appalled.

The gathering storm nearer to home was paralleled by a darkening in his own life. The ten years of freedom he desired were all he was to be granted, as gradually and inexorably his health began to break down. Malaria, a legacy of West African ports, recurred sporadically.

Britain's declaration of war on Nazi Germany in September 1939 found the Lowe family willing to serve. Harold Jr enlisted in the Royal Engineers. Lowe offered his home as a sector post for operations in the Deganwy area. He also took up duties as an air raid warden. His son joined a generation readying for war and would soon depart for India with the Royal Bombay Sappers and Miners, commanding H Company. While stationed in Halifax, he met a young nurse, Marguerite 'Peggy' Davies, and the two became close before Harold's departure overseas. Before he left they became engaged, and in his absence his fiancée became close to the remaining Lowe family.

Thirty years had gone by since that night in 1912. The tide of war had ebbed from British shores and moved east, to Russia, the Pacific,

Pearl Harbor. The maps were still spread out in the potting shed, the trench-telescope set firmly on the church clock but Lowe no longer had to patrol the streets to urge residents to extinguish every tiny glimmer that might give comfort to the Luftwaffe. And then a light suddenly went out. The hands on the church clock seemed to momentarily stand still. A small part of a small world shuddered briefly. Harold Lowe collapsed with a cerebral stroke, just as had his grandfather Thomas Quick.

The blow, in 1942, caused immediate, if only partial, paralysis. The man of action was turned instantly to a man of hesitation and infirmity. His movements were severely restricted with no possibility of recovery, and his last voyage – the most personal of all – would be made in a wheelchair.

For a man of Lowe's boundless energy and activity the physical incapacity must have been almost unendurable. Nellie, who had spent so long nursing her father, gently embraced the task of caring for her husband, supported by Josie and Peggy. His hard fought-for self control came to the forefront and for the most part he contained the irritation and even anger that he must have felt.

He developed a rapport with Peggy, appreciating the time she spent with him trying to share some of his interests, although communication for him was difficult. He attempted to teach her how to use a sextant and navigational tools, 'but that was a bit of a dead loss,' she fondly recalled.[108]

Nellie and Peggy would wheel Lowe down the Promenade, and along by the river. To please him, they took him to the moored *Pirate*, still waiting for her master. But a lifetime had all but gone by, and he was far from those vessels he had loved and served, commanded and obeyed in turn. The reefing of sails, the reading of chart and cloud and compass, all was behind him. The sea was ever the sea, regal and compelling, but now he was relegated to role of mere observer. In his broken state, his bodily entrapment, he still loved to gaze on the sea's face. Nellie would wait patiently, silently, behind his wheelchair until he was ready to go.

Once he might have expected to pass in storm, or war, or accident. Such had nearly happened on several occasions. It had taken luck, or courage, or quick thinking to survive. Brother seamen and officers had not been so fortunate, nor his own brothers, all of them brothers of the sea. Harold Lowe died at home with Nellie on 12 May 1944.

The passing was marked in local papers, the *Barmouth Advertiser* reporting, 'Death of Commander Lowe. He was on the *Titanic.*' The obituary touched briefly on his civic role, the First World War, and early seafaring career, but it was the *Titanic* that earned the column inches. Lowe was the first of the surviving officers to die.

At the next Conwy Borough Council meeting, the mayor's resolution of sympathy for Ellen and the family members in their bereavement would be carried by the members standing.

Harold Jr was not at home, but in the jungle. He fought on unawares, soon to be wounded on long-range penetration in Burma.

A short funeral service was conducted in the Lowe home on 16 May. The coffin was draped in the Union Jack, surmounted by trappings of the Royal Naval Reserve in ceremonial sword, hat and medals. His brother Freemasons conducted their own rites at the graveside.

Nellie had chosen interment in the seaside churchyard of Llandrillo yn Rhos, where her parents were buried, close to Bryn Mostyn where she and Harold had shared their early married life. She had preferred the convention of a churchyard interment rather than that of a cemetery, and her husband would no doubt have been in accord.

The headstone, when erected, gave only his name, RNR rank, age and date of death, and no shadow of the *Titanic* fell across it. But it also included words of love for 'my devoted husband' – 'I thank my God upon every remembrance of you.'

From the graveside, visitors can lift their eyes from the grave of Harold Lowe to look out over the serried crosses, past the Little Orme, to a glimpse of the sea beyond.

EPILOGUE

For many years the story ended in the churchyard of Llandrillo yn Rhos. Nell, always strong, ever competent, continued her active community roles, serving as president of the local Electrical Association for Women and a supporter of All Saints church and the local hospital. But she too was to fall victim to heart disease, and after a brief illness of a few days died at home three years after her husband, and was buried beside him. Her own inscription on the facing side of the book-shaped headstone recalled the sacrifices and sorrows she had endured in her life: 'Oh generous heart...'

The grass grows long around their grave in the summer months, but there are now many friendly and admiring hands to trim it back and lay flowers. The story of how Harold emerged from near-obscurity at the time of his death to a form of international recognition is part of the tale. While the rest of the world largely forgot him, a memory of Lowe's strong personality lingered in Deganwy. The boys who had played along the stretch of beach in front of his home grew to manhood still vividly remembering his formidable presence and how he had seemed the lord of that small world. The impression of his character remained with those who had known him, just as the familiar, homely smell of his favourite strong tobacco hung in the smoking room of his house for many years after his death.

The publication of Walter Lord's *A Night to Remember* in 1955 led to some revival of interest in the fifth officer, and the lines of the legend began to re-emerge; the colourful officer was revived on paper. 'A tempestuous young Welshman,' wrote Lord, 'Lowe was hard to suppress.'[109] When the book came to the screen, Lowe's character, played by Howard Pays, lost his dramatic confrontation with Ismay to Kenneth More's Lightoller. He was left, however, with a strong scene in the lifeboats; after announcing they were to return for survivors, he silenced a crewmember protesting that they were overcrowded with a curt, 'Rubbish! You've room for about 20 more in that boat. Now hold your tongue and do as you're told.' It was a fleeting moment, but the outline of character and incident were recognisable.

It was author Wyn Craig Wade who was to restore Lowe to prominence in the story. His *Titanic, End of a Dream*, published in 1979, painted a memorable picture of the man who, he opined, was 'the most conscientious officer and best all-around sailor aboard.'[110] Dealing primarily with Lowe's role in loading the lifeboats, his blunt-spoken, honest seaman emerged in strong if over-simplified colours. He dominates sections of the book, just as Lowe's testimony provided reams of rich newsprint in 1912. Wade was also the first *Titanic* author to delve beyond Lowe's brief self-portrait given at the American inquiry and provide a few details of his career pre- and post-*Titanic*, drawn mainly from his obituary.

Lowe had several screen incarnations after his appearance in *A Night to Remember*. In *SOS Titanic* (1979) he was played by Karl Howman. He was recreated by Kavan Smith for a fairly substantial role in the CBS miniseries *Titanic* (1996) and was also given screen time in the 1984 German made-for-television movie of the same name. The two latter productions owed much to Wade's work, and presented the young officer as a plainspoken man of the sea. All three had a focus on the Ismay incident, and the German telemovie – which used the American inquiry as the frame for a courtroom-style drama – showed a confident, even over-confident young man smirking his way through his testimony and playing the crowd for laughs.

In 1997 the revival of interest in this obscure merchant officer that began with Wade's work reached a new height. As Lord's *A Night to Remember* and the discovery of the wreck in 1985 led to renewed interest in the disaster, the public's fascination with the ship surged in 1997 with the release of James Cameron's film *Titanic*, an epic centred around fictional characters Rose deWitt Bukater and Jack Dawson. Cameron cast a good-looking but then unknown young Welsh actor, RADA graduate Ioan Gruffudd, in the role of the fifth officer. While the Ismay confrontation was again filmed, it did not make the final cut. What did make the final version were the shots at Boat 14 and the heartbreaking poignancy of Boat 14's return to search for survivors. One can quibble with the historical details – Lowe is shown with an electric torch that had long since given out in reality, encountering the body of a dead woman and baby in spite of his categorical denial that he saw any women in the wreckage – but one cannot argue with the emotional veracity of the scene. As

Lowe and his crew row through a field of bodies, the officer breathes in frustration and agonised regret that 'we waited too long'.

The older incarnation of the film's heroine tells the audience in a voiceover that, '… only one went back. *One*.' That phrase helped cement the legend that Boat 14 was the only lifeboat to return and confirmed Lowe's place in the pantheon of canonical *Titanic* heroes.

In an apotheosis he could never have imagined, Lowe was represented as a 'Rescue Bear' collectable toy, and he was celebrated on a Maldives postal stamp with his name alongside a White Star Line officer's uniform button. A Welsh film crew produced a documentary on his life, filmed on location in Barmouth and narrated by Ioan Gruffudd. Produced with the working title *Y Cymro Ag Aeth Yn Ól* (*The Welshman Who Went Back*) it aired in Wales on New Year's Eve 2001 as *The Real Hero of the Titanic*, which would have delighted Rene Harris. In 2004, the menu that Lowe had sent Nellie from the *Titanic* fetched a record auction price of £52,000. Media releases from auctioneers Henry Aldridge and Son described Lowe as 'undoubtedly the real hero of the disaster.' As this book nears completion, plans are afoot for the unveiling of a memorial to Lowe in Barmouth to mark the centennial of the *Titanic* disaster, and more documentaries are planned. Nearly seventy years after his death, Harold Lowe's story has once again captured the imagination of the world.

Affidavit of
Harold Lowe

In the Matter
Of the
Investigation into the Loss of the
Steamship Titanic

HAROLD GODFREY LOWE, being duly sworn, deposes and states as follows:

My name is Harold Godfrey Lowe. My home is Pennrallt, Bormouth, England [sic]. I will be 29 years old the Fall of this year.

I joined the Titanic at Belfast in the capacity of fifth officer on the 29th March, 1912. I hold an ordinary master's certificate of competency, issue by the British Board of Trade about 4 years ago, and the number I cannot at the present moment remember.

While the ship was at Belfast, lying fast alongside the wharf, at the direction of Mr. Murdoch, who was then chief officer, I in company with Mr Moody, the sixth officer, inspected all the lifeboats, emergency boats and collapsible boats on the starboard side, together with their equipment.

On the starboard side, there were seven lifeboats, one emergency boat and two collapsibles. The seven lifeboats rested on chocks under the davits with the falls attached. The emergency boat was hanging outboard on falls from davits. One of the collapsibles was resting on the deck that held the davits that held the emergency boat, and the other collapsible was directly opposite this and on top of the officers' quarters.

There was a set and a half of oars in each lifeboat. In each of the lifeboats there were a mast, sail rigging, and tarpaulin bag to hold the same. There were a double set of thole pins and one veering rowlock. There were a rudder and tiller and a rudder-rope, a painter, a sea anchor, bailers and breakers. There were two waterbreakers in each of the lifeboats, and one in the emergency boat. One bread tank in each of the lifeboats and in the emergency boats. I do not remember whether there were any bread tanks in the collapsibles. I do not remember whether there were any water breakers or bread tanks in the collapsibles. I do not remember whether there were water breakers when I inspected them in Belfast; and there was no bread in the bread tanks when I inspected them at Belfast. But such of the bread tanks and water breakers as I saw in the Carpathia subsequently after the accident did contain bread and water.

I cannot remember having seen any lanterns in the lifeboats when I inspected them at Belfast. I do not know of my own knowledge whether there were any lifeboat lanterns on board the ship. After the lifeboats had been taken on board the Carpathia, I remember having seen some lanterns taken from some of the lifeboats, but which I cannot remember, nor how many.

There were no liferafts on board the Titanic. There were life buoys on board. There were life belts placed in every room on board.

On the trials the Titanic behaved splendidly and manoeuvred very well.

We sailed from Belfast on the 1st, and got to Southampton about the 3rd. While the ship was lying alongside the dock at Southampton the whole deck department was mustered, and two of the lifeboats on the starboard side were manned and lowered away. I myself taking charge of one and the sixth taking charge of the other. This is the only time that I saw a boat drill take place on the Titanic.

After leaving Queenstown, Mr. Murdock [sic], the first officer, made out a boat list, stationing the men at their different positions at the boats, and there was an emergency boat list made out as well. I cannot say definitely whether either or both of these lists were posted in the forecastle. I do not now remember to what boat I had been assigned on this list. The general boat list passed through my hands in being sent to the captain for approval. I glanced at this list casually, and remember form this glance that that there were three seamen assigned to some of the boats and four to others.

We left Southampton at about 12:05 p.m. on Wednesday, April 10th, and arrived at Cherbourg in the same evening. We sailed for Queenstown from Cherbourg the same evening, and we arrived at Queenstown the following morning. We sailed from Queenstown about 2:30 the same afternoon.

All went well from Queenstown until Sunday, April 14th. We had fine, clear weather and smooth sea.

During my watch from 6 to 8 I noticed that a chit had been placed on the officers' chart room table. There was written on the chit the word 'Ice' and the position underneath. I cannot remember what the position of the ice was. So far as I can remember, I figured it out roughly mentally and found that we would not come within the limits of the ice regions during my watch.

At the beginning of each watch the junior officer relieving the deck would immediately ring up the engine room and get the revolutions for the last watch. I did this several times during the voyage, and the highest number of revolutions which I remember being reported to me from the engine room was about 74. During my watch from 6 to 8 the engine room telegraph indicated full speed ahead. The night was fine and clear, bright overhead and dark on the water; calm wind and sea. I did not particularly notice that it was very cold during the watch on deck. As near as I can remember, the barometer during the watch would be about 29.80. I went below at 8 o'clock, undressed, turned in, and went to sleep.

The next thing I remember was hearing voices. It must have been just about midnight. I half woke up; I was not fully awake; and I listened; and after listening awhile I got up and opened the door and looked out on the deck, and saw passengers with life-belts on and the crew clearing away the boats. I dressed and went to the starboard side, and assisted in getting over No.7 lifeboat on the starboard side. I cannot remember whether all the seamen on the starboard side were engaged in working No.7 lifeboat. I know that we worked the lifeboats one by one, and that before we proceeded to No.5 lifeboat some men had cut off the covers. I cannot say definitely, or give any estimate for, the number of seamen on this side of the ship at this time.

We succeeded in lowering away No.7, after having filled it with women and children and placed four men in it as well for a crew. I do not know whether these four men were seamen, or firemen, or stewards, or what they were.

Then I proceeded to No.5 lifeboat and loaded it in a similar fashion, and then No.3, and then the emergency boat, placing

women and children in each of them until all the women and
children that were on that side of the deck had gone. In No.3
and the emergency boat we put men as well as women. The
ship at this time was tipping rather badly, but she had no list that
I noticed.

I then proceeded to the port side, and found sixth officer
Moody filling boat No.16 with women and children. I stated to
Moody that I had seen five boats go away without a responsible
person in them, meaning by this an officer. And I asked him who
it was to be, him or I, to go in the boat, he said 'You go. I will get
away in some other boat.'

I went in Boat 14. That was the boat that I was loading. Boats
Nos. 16, 14 and 12 were loaded much about the same time.

I saw no confusion whatever, either in the handling, loading or
lowering, of either the boats on the starboard or on the port side.

I took two boats away with me; that is, excluding my own.
I was in Boat 14. I took them to a distance of about 150 yards
from the ship. I then returned and escorted another boat to the
other two boats. I then returned again to the ship and escorted
a collapsible to these other three boats. I then made all the boats
make fast to each other fore and aft, and also made them all set
their masts ready for any emergency, such as wind. I then tied my
own boat at the head of the string of boats.

The ship by this time was settling down rapidly by the head,
and sank in about 20 minutes. The lights were burning up to 5
minutes before the stern disappeared. I did not hear anything that
I should call explosions. I kind of distant smothered rumblings.
I thought at the time it was produced by the sinking of the ship.

As I was putting over the starboard emergency boat somebody
mentioned something about a ship on the port bow. I glanced
in that direction and saw a steamer showing her red light about
5 miles to the northward of us.

At this time fourth officer Boxhill [sic] was firing off signals
of distress, and we also Morsed to the ship by the electric Morse
lamps on the bridge.

When I had got these boats tied together I still saw these in the
same position, and shortly afterward she seemed to alter her position and open her green. I knew a few minutes afterwards all the
lights went out, and I did not see any more lights until I saw the
lights of the Carpathia.

The cries of the drowning people had very much subsided, and I thought it was safe to venture in amongst them; and to do this I had to transfer all my 58 passengers from my boat into the other 4 boats, and I evenly distributed them into the other four boats; and then went away with an empty boat with just a boat's crew and no passengers. I searched the wreck thoroughly and found four persons, three of whom survived, and one died on board my boat.

During this time I was under sail, and, as I was sailing away from the wreckage, I saw the collapsible which was in my charge, and I sailed down to her and took her in tow. She was in a pretty bad condition, because a breeze had sprung up and there was some sea, and she was somewhat overcrowded because I transferred my passengers.

Whilst towing this collapsible boat I noticed another collapsible boat, which had been pierced by wreckage and was settling fast; and I sailed down to her and took off approximately 20 men and 1 woman. I then made for the Carpathia, and we were picked up by her.

In the morning I saw a number of male bodies floating about. They all had lifebelts on. I did not see a single female body.

The wreckage that was floating about consisted of tables, chairs, blankets, settees and other wood furniture.

There were not compasses on any of the lifeboats, so far as I can say.

As Boat 14, of which I had charge, was being lowered two dark complexioned men tried to jump into the boat. One of them succeeded, and I threw him out; and then, to prevent any repetition of the occurrence, I fired my revolver in the air as I passed each deck.

Signed and sworn to at the
British Consulate General
New York this   day [sic]
Of May, 1912, before me

CAREER HISTORY
OF HAROLD LOWE

Date	Rank	Ship	Line	Destination
c.1898		Schooner		Welsh Coast
		Schooner		Welsh Coast
		Schooner		Welsh Coast
		Schooner		Welsh Coast
c. 1900	OS	*Merrion Lass*		Welsh Coast
28/05/1900 – 30/10/1900	OS	*William Keith*		Ireland/Wales
22/01/1901 – 18/06/1901	OS	*British Queen*		
21/06/1901 – 04/04/1902	AB	*Cortez*		Iquique
20/05/1902 – 28/01/1903	OS	*Balasore*		
11/03/1903 – 27/05/1904	AB	*Ormsary*		Australia
27/05/04 – 06/08/04	Rating	On Drill RNR		
06/08/04 – 21/11/04	AB	SS *Prometheus*	Alfred Holt	
1 March 1905 – Board of Trade Inquiry witness				
05/03/05 – 12/10/1905	AB	SS *Telemachus*	Alfred Holt	Seattle via Japan
01/06	Sits for Second Mate's Certificate – Fails			
17/02/06 – 06/05/06	AB	SS *Justin*	J.R. Ellerman	
29/05/06 – 23/07/06	AB	SS *Fabian*	J.R. Ellerman	Mediterranean Ports
20/08/06	Passes Second Mate's Certificate			

Date	Rank	Ship	Line	Destination
03/10/06 – 03/12/06	3/Officer	SS *Ardeoloa*	Yeoward Brothers	Canary Islands
19/12/06 – 15/03/07	4/Officer	SS *Chama*	Elder Dempster	West Africa
06/07/07 – 15/04/08	3/Officer	SS *Bonny*	Elder Dempster	West Africa
20/07/08	Sits for First Mate's Certificate – Fails			
29/07/08	Sits for Second Mate's Certificate – Passes			
09/09/1908 –	2/Officer – C/Officer	SS *Madeira*	Elder Dempster	West Africa
17/12/1908		SS *Oron*	Elder Dempster	West Africa
1/06/1909 – 14/08/1910		SS *Addah*	Elder Dempster	West Africa
26/10/1910	Sits for Master's Certificate – Fails			
7/11/1910	Sits for Master's Certificate – Passes			
10/12/1910 – 18/03/1911		SS *Zaria*	Elder Dempster	West Africa
22/04/1911 – 19/09/1911	3/Officer	SS *Tropic*	White Star Line	Australia
22/09/1911 – 21/02/1912	3/Officer	SS *Belgic*	White Star Line	Australia
24/03/1912 – 15/04/1912	5/Officer	RMS *Titanic*	White Star Line	New York
03/08/1912 – 01/12/1912	3/Officer	RMS *Medic*	White Star Line	Australia
20/12/1912 – 12/04/1913	3/Officer	SS *Gothic*	White Star Line	Australia
09/07/1913 – 26/02/1914	2/Officer	SS *Cornishman*		Montreal (6 voyages)
c. 03/1914	Sub-Lieut	HMS *Hogue* [?]	RNR	
03/04/1914	Sub-Lieut	HMS *Excellent*	RNR	
06/04/1914	Sub-Lieut	HMS *Victory*	RNR	
20/07/1915	Promoted to Lieutenant			
02/01/1916 – 30/03/1917	Lieut	HMS *Donegal*	RNR	Patrolling

Date	Rank	Ship	Line	Destination
01/04/1917	Lieut	HMS *Victory*	RNR	
17/05/1917 -10/06/1919	Lieut	HMS *Suffolk*	RNR	
20/11/1919 – 29/12/1912	1/Officer	SS *Turcoman*	Frederick Leyland	Portland
09/01/1920 – 26/04/1920	2/Officer	SS *Cedric*	White Star Line	New York (2 voyages)
18/08/1920 – 08/04/1921	1/Officer	SS *Dominion*	Dominion Line	Quebec, Montreal, New York and Portland
12/11/1921 – 26/11/1921	Lieut	HMS *Defiance*	RNR	Torpedo School Ship
26/11/1921	Lieut	HMS *Vivid*	RNR	Shoreside Training
13/05/1922 – 27/12/1925	C/Officer	SS *Gallic*	White Star Line	Australia and New Zealand (7 voyages)
20/11/1923	Promoted to Commander RNR			
03/04/1925 – 24/05/1925	1/Officer & C/Officer	SS *Canada*	Leyland Line	Portland, Maine and Montreal (2 voyages)
01/08/1925 – 09/08/1925	1/Officer	SS *Suevic*	White Star Line	Glasgow
14/08/1925 – 15/08/1926 ★	2/Officer	SS *Regina*	Leyland	Montreal and New York (11 voyages)
29/01/1927 – 12/12/1927	2/Officer	SS *Ceramic*	White Star Line	Australia (2 voyages)
04/02/1928 – 28/02/1928	2/Officer	SS *Regina*	White Star Line	New York
03/03/1928 – 26/03/1928	2/Officer	SS *Baltic*	White Star Line	New York
04/1928		SS *Laurentic*	White Star Line	Canada
27/07/1928 – 1931	2/Officer – 1/Officer	SS *Doric*	White Star Line	Canada

ENDNOTES

1 'The Late Mr Quick', *The Daily Post*, 7 December 1867

2 'Fatal Boating Accident on the Estuary', *Barmouth and County Advertiser*, 8 August 1894

3 *Barmouth and County Advertiser*, 1 January 1896

4 Lowe, H.G., Am. Inq., p.369

5 Lowe, H.W.G., letter to Kerri Sundberg, 13 October 1998

6 Lowe, H.W.G., letter to Kerri Sundberg, 13 October 1998

7 Roberts, G., 'The Autobiography of Griffith Roberts', *Maritime Wales No.7*, 1984, p.131

8 Roberts, D., 'Captain Robert Davies of the Kirkcudbrightshire', *Maritime Wales No.8*, 1984, p.56

9 Service, R., *Collected poems of Robert Service*, G.P. Putnam's Sons, New York, p.464

10 Lowe, H.W.G., letter to the author, 10 August 1998

11 Moody, J.P., letter, 11 January 1906

12 Moody, J.P., letter to Margaret Moody, 23 January 1908

13 Lightoller, C.H., *Titanic and Other Ships*, Ivor Nicholson and Watson, London, 1936, p.91

14 *The Shipping Gazette Weekly Summary*, 3 March 1905

15 *Barmouth and County Advertiser*, 25 April 1912

16 *Ibid.*

17 Bisset, J., *Tramps and Ladies*, Patrick Stephens Limited, Bath, 1988, p.146

18 Hayman, S., cited in Cowden, J., Duffy, J., *The Elder Dempster Fleet History 1852–1985*, Mallett and Bell, 1986, University of Virginia, p.67

19 Hough, Captain G., reference for Harold Lowe, 14 August 1910 (John Creamer collection)

20 *The Colwyn Bay Herald*, 30 July 1908

21 *The Advertiser*, Adelaide, 20 November 1911, Retrieved from the National Library of Australia website, http://trove.nla.gov.au/news-paper

22 *The West Australian*, 13 November 1911, Retrieved from the National Library of Australia website, http://newspapers.nla.gov.au/

23 *The Advertiser*, Adelaide, 20 November 1911, Retrieved from the National Library of Australia website, http://trove.nla.gov.au/news-paper

24 Moody, J.P., letter to Margaret Moody, 21 March 1912

25 Moody, J.P., letter 29 March 1912

26 Lowe, H.G., *US Senate Sub-Committee Hearings*, p.376

27 White Star Line Special Meeting, 22 April 1912, Minute No.8424 Reprinted in *The Commutator*, Vol.22, No.4, Feb–April 1999, p.28

28 Moody, J.P., letter, 29 March 1912

29 Moody, J.P., letter, 29 March 1912

30 Moody, J.P., letter to Margaret Moody, 21 March 1912

31 Marcus, G., *The Maiden Voyage*, Viking Press, New York, 1969, p.58

32 Marcus, *Ibid.*, pp.82–3

33 Villiers, A., *Of Ships and Men. A Personal Anthology, London*, 1962 p.124

34 Smith, J., letter to Hugh Smith April 1912, *Northern Constitution*, 11 May 1912

35 Moody, J.P., letter, 18 February 1905

36 Moody, J.P., letter to Margaret Moody, 4 April 1912

37 Moody, J.P., letter to Margaret Moody, 4 April 1912

38 Moody, J.P., postcard to Ellen Whitehouse, 5 April 1912

39 Lowe, H.G., affidavit, May 1912 (John Creamer collection)

40 Statement of Harold Godfrey Lowe, sworn at Hill Dickinson & Co., Liverpool 1912 (John Creamer collection)

41 Walcroft, N., *Maidenhead Advertiser*, 29 April 1912, Cameron, C., letter, 21 April 1912

42 Stengel, C.E.H., US Senate Sub-Committee Hearings, 30 April 1912, p.975

43 White, E., US Senate Sub-Committee Hearings, 2 May 1912, p.1008

44 Stengel, C., US Senate Sub-Committee Hearings, 30 April 1912, p.975

45 Chambers, N., Am. Inq., p.1044

46 Lowe, H.G., Am. Inq., 24 April 1912, p.389

47 Simpson, L., letter, 8 October 1912 (Nornan collection)

48 Lowe, H.G., Am. Inq., 24 April 1912, p.399

49 Br. Inq. Qs.15908–11

50 Cameron, C., letter to Janet Dowding, 30[?] May 1912

51 *Newport Herald*, 30 May 1912; Lowe, H.G. Am. Inq. p. 400

52 Cameron, C., letter to Janet Dowding, 21 April 1912

53 Collyer, C., *The Semi-Monthly Magazine*, May 1912

54 *Ibid.*

55 Threlfall, T., interview, *The Bridgewater Mercury*, May 1912

56 Cameron, C., letter to Janet Dowding, 21 April 1912

57 Haisman, D., son of Edith Haisman via email to author 23 February 2001

58 Clench, F., Am. Inq., p.636

59 Compton, S., cited in Gracie, A., *Titanic, A Survivor's Story*, Academy Chicago, 1996, p.171 (originally published as *The Truth About the Titanic*, 1913)

60 Harris, R., *New York Evening Journal*, 11 May 1912

61 Pitman, H., Am. Inq., p.282

62 Ryerson, E., Am Inq., p.1108

63 Crowe, G.F., Am. Inq., p.616

64 Unidentified *Titanic* crewman, *The Western Mercury*, 29 April 1912

65 Cameron, C., letter to Janet Dowding, 21 April 1912

66 Minahan, D., Am Inq., p.1109

67 Harris, R, *New York Evening Journal*, 11 May 1912

68 Cameron, C., letter to Janet Dowding, 29 April 1912; Compton, p.169; Haisman, D., via email to author, 23 February 2001

69 Lowe, H.G., affidavit, May 1912 (John Creamer collection)

70 Collyer, C., *The Semi-Monthly Magazine*, May 1912

71 Joseph Scarrott (1912) 'An account of the Titanic disaster by a survivor' *The Sphere* (ref: #12677, accessed 19th September 2011 03:43:24 AM), http://www.encyclopedia-titanica.org/an-account-of-the-titanic-disaster-by-a-survivor.html

72 Cameron, C., letter to Janet Dowding, 30[?] May 1912

73 Harris, R., *New York Evening Journal*, 11 May 1912

74 Rheims, G., letter to wife 19 April 1912, cited Encyclopaedia Titanica Articles [www.encyclopedia-titanica.org], accessed 23 February 14:21:01 2003

75 Harris, R., *New York Evening Journal*, 11 May 1912

76 Lowe, H.G., Am. Inq., p.412

77 Lowe, H.G., Am. Inq., p.402

78 Lowe, H.W.G., letter to author, 10 August 1998

79 *The Evening News*, Saulte Ste Marie, 24 April 1912

80 *Newport Herald*, 30 May 1912

81 Cameron, C., letter to Janet Dowding, 30 May 1912

82 Threlfall, T., interview, *The Bridgewater Mercury*, May 1912

83 Following quotations unless otherwise indicated are from the Am. Inq.,
    pp.368–421

84 Bayliss, J.E., letter to Harold Lowe, 20 May 1912

85 *The Providence Daily Journal*, cited by Gowan, P.&B. Meister &
    B. Holmer, *Titanic Woman of Sorrows*; http://www.titanic-titanic.com/
    articles/phil_gowan_bio_rhoda_abbott.shtml accessed 27 January
    2005

86 Harris, R., *New York Evening Journal*, 11 May 1912

87 Cameron, C., letter to Janet Dowding 30[?] May 1912

88 Harris, R., 'Her Husband Went Down With The Titanic', *Liberty*
    magazine, 23 April 1932

89 Bayliss, J.E., letter to Harold Lowe, 20 May 1912

90 *Daily Express*, 29 April 1912

91 Moody, J.P., postcard to Margaret Moody, 1 April 1912

92 Simpson, L., letter, 8 October 1912, Dornan Collection

93 *The Sydney Morning Herald*, 14 February 1913

94 Lowe, H.G., letter to Selena Rogers Cook, 14 March 1913, *The
    Commutator*, vol.22, No.4 Feb–April 1999, p.14

95 Diary of Herbert Simpkins, Royal Naval Museum Manuscript
    Collection, 2000/81

96 Lifschitz, J.A., pamphlet collected by Harold G. Lowe in Vladivostok,
    1918

97 Williams, A.R., *Through the Russian Revolution*, Bonar and Liveright,
    1921, p.246

98 Williams, *Ibid.*, p.250

99 Official Log of HMS *Suffolk*, PRO ADM 53/61631

100 Telegram 143, British High Commission Vladivostok to Foreign Office,
    4 February 1919, FO 267/1421 National Archives

101 Diary of Herbert Simpkins, Royal Naval Museum Manuscript
    Collection 2000/81

102 Lowe, H.W.G., interview with author

103 Lowe, H.W.G., letter to author, 9 August 1998

104 Lowe, H.W.G., letter to Dowding, E.&D., 13 February 1998

105 Lowe, H.W.G., letter to author, 10 August 1998

106 Lowe, J., letter to author, 26 May 1998

107 Lowe, H.W.G., letter to author, 10 August 1998

108 Lowe, M., interview with author

109 Lord, W., *A Night to Remember*, Penguin Books revised illustrated edition, London, 1976, p.70

110 Wade, W.C., *The Titanic: End of a Dream*, Penguin Books revised edition 1986, New York, p.197

111 Lowe, H.G., affidavit, May 1912 (John Creamer collection)

THE TITANIC COLLECTION

THE 100TH ANNIVERSARY OF THE SINKING OF TITANIC 15TH APRIL 2012

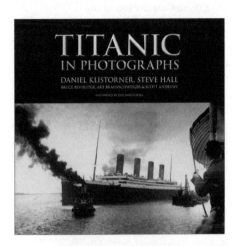

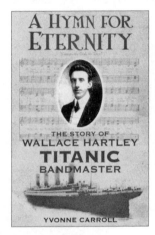

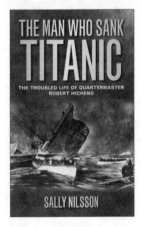

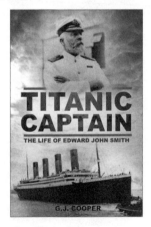